WATER
A DREAM I

Ursula Maddy

Waterperry
GARDENS
01844 339226

First published in Great Britain, 1990
Reprinted in Great Britain 2001
Reprinted in Great Britain 2018

British Library Cataloguing in Publication Data
Maddy, Ursula
Waterperry.
1. Oxfordshire. Waterperry. Horticultural colleges.
Waterperry Horticultural School, history
I. Title
635.071142579

ISBN 0-86303-502-7

ISBN 0 86303 502-7

Printed and bound by CPI Group (UK) Ltd, Croydon, CR0 4YY

For Miss H. and Miss S.,
For Jean and Mary
who kept their dream alive,
And for all
who have played any part in
their story

Acknowledgements

This history is an attempt to answer the frequent question, "How did it all start?" and to put on record a unique venture. At Beatrix Havergal's death her papers were unceremoniously dumped into boxes for the Oxford County Records Office and I spent many happy hours there sorting through them.

I am deeply indebted to Christopher Havergal for illuminating glimpses of Beatrix Havergal's childhood and family life. Cynthia Havergal put her cousin's later correspondence at my disposal, and the late Joan Sanders talked with me about her sister Avice. From Peggy Fonge I had an eye-witness account of Pusey and the move to Waterperry, and her help was invaluable. I am also grateful to Annelise Burkhardt-Reinhardt for permission to use her letters. Any attempt to list former students who helped would result in a roll call; I hope they will recognize their contributions and accept my thanks. For Oxford Shop memories I am especially grateful to Irene Collins and Honor Shorten, while Barbara Kitson, always generous to Waterperry, has been most helpful and encouraging. Mary Spiller has read several chapters, corrected errors and made valuable suggestions while Jean Manger, who has lived with the project as it developed, has been a constant help and support. Indebted as I am to so many for information I must stress that any opinions expressed are entirely my own. Finally I thank Mary R. Price for so much help; she has been guide, philospher and friend throughout.

Contents

Illustrations

Set between pp.80 and 81

Introduction

Five miles east of Oxford along the A40 road to London there is a turn-off to the left with a sign saying 'Waterperry Gardens'. If you follow this sign, skirt the village of Wheatley, and then take a winding road for another two miles you come to Waterperry village. At the furthest point of the village are the gardens.

At first you may appear to have arrived at just another Garden Centre, and for many it is enough to browse contentedly among the plants and shrubs for sale, the seed packets and the soil mixtures. But those who venture beyond the shop through an archway of mellow brick find themselves in a beautiful garden surrounding both a fine old house and a small ancient church. It is not an unusual complex to find in an English village, but this garden is quite different from others in that it was developed for a special purpose and is the birthplace of a remarkable enterprise created by a remarkable woman, Beatrix Havergal.

Ursula Maddy was born on a Cotswold farm. She trained in Physical Education during the War, teaching in girls' grammar schools before going up to Durham University to read Theology. Ursula started working for Miss Havergal as a casual labourer and eventually became a full member of staff.

She was an organist in Waterperry Church and in Holton for many years and Secretary of the Waterperry PCC for 24 years.

Her interests include literature, music and horse-racing.

Chapter One

Grace Beatrix Helen Havergal was born on 7th July, 1901, at Royden Manor House near Bressingham in Norfolk, the second child of the Revd Clement Havergal, the Vicar of Bressingham. This formidable array of feminine names was almost instantly reduced to Charlie Trix, a doubtful compliment perhaps in those more gracious days but one which must have suited the sturdy little girl. Early photographs show a lively broad-browed child, more boyish than girlish, obviously full of energy and ready to face the world. 'Charlie' was gradually dropped, the affectionate 'Trix' remained. She already had an elder sister, Frances; the adored younger brother, Christopher, was not born until 1907.

A Victorian parsonage is usually thought of as a sheltered and totally stable environment, not so Royden Manor. Trix's father, the Revd Clement, came of a gifted clerical line; his father, the Revd Henry East Havergal, Vicar of Cople, Bedfordshire, had been a noted musician and carpenter, while his grandfather, William Henry Havergal, Honorary Canon of Worcester, was a composer of church music whose memorial can be found in the south-east transept of Worcester Cathedral. Probably a greater influence still was that of his aunt, Frances Ridley Havergal, sixth and youngest child of William Henry who in her short life, 1836-79, wrote some of the most splendid, if now unfashionable, hymns in the Anglican repertoire. Janet Grierson, in her excellent life of Frances Ridley Havergal, records that Henry East Havergal's death aroused in the hymn writer a sense of special responsibility for the eighteen-year-old nephew, Clement. He had already announced his intention of going into the Church, giving rise to this reaction from Frances in a letter: 'So interested about Clement — thankful there seems one spiritually minded MALE Havergal. May all the rest follow.' Clearly she intended the furthering of Clement's vocation to be important in her own life. Frances Ridley Havergal's deeply held religious convictions, her musical talents and passionate love of nature, her unconventionality — she was a fearless Alpinist and once threw off all but her petticoat to make an ascent —

found echoes in her great niece, even in the tensions of a difficult family life. Frances Ridley's mother died when she was eleven, and the relationship with her stepmother was never happy.

Trix's family life was not unhappy, far from it, but it was, by the standards of the day, unstable. The Havergals, as a family, appear as artistic, energetic, given to magnificent enthusiasms, and perhaps a little larger than life. The Revd Clement channelled his gifts into becoming, "An exceedingly eccentric character to say the least of it", according to his son, while his churchmanship narrowed to an uncompromising Calvinistic attitude, repressive in the extreme. Mrs Havergal, twelve years his junior, also held strong religious views but these were romantically and artistically expressed. She had trained as a painter in both watercolour and oil and had had some pictures accepted for the Royal Academy exhibitions. Obviously the difference in temperament between the two parents led to a potentially explosive atmosphere.

Perhaps because of this sunshine-and-storm climate the Revd Clement was very restless. When Trix was one year old he moved to Inkberrow, near Redditch. The following two years were spent as Assistant Chaplain to the British Embassy in Paris, then there was a short stay at Bagthorpe. At last he settled as Rector of Brent Eleigh in Suffolk where he remained until his final retirement.

A highly eccentric and dour father matched with an artistically and romantically inclined mother may not make for stability in a family, but it is quite certain that they do not make for boredom and Brent Eleigh Rectory must have been a lively and stimulating home. Here Trix grew up somewhat in the shadow of her sister Frances, two years older and different in every respect. Frances was petite, exceedingly pretty, feminine, academically inclined and industrious, whereas Trix was large, handsome, tomboyish, good with her hands and naughty. It seems obvious that Frances dominated her younger sister and must often have been held up to her as a model, a model that Trix had neither the physical attributes nor the mental application to emulate. It was perhaps in these early days that seeds of insecurity were laid in Trix, and insecurity which for all her later success she never quite overcame, and which made her often rely on others to make important decisions.

Life at Brent Eleigh, in spite of its problems, must have been fun, fun remaining one of Trix's key expressions throughout her life. A large rambling rectory, no doubt uncomfortable by present standards but surrounded by spacious gardens, trees, and stables with lofts, was an ideal home for a tomboy who already would seem to have shown an interest in growing things. On her sixth birthday presents from her grandmother included 'a little box of tins for you to keep shop with, and the water can to feed the flowers with.' Her brother, Christopher, had been born a month before, and Mrs Havergal and the baby were away recuperating from what had been a difficult time. Frances had been sent away earlier so that Trix was left to romp alone. Her 'little Grandma', for so she styles herself, wrote that she knew Trix was longing to see her mother and the baby back but her mother must get stronger first. Trix was to remember Jesus' words about little children, and she was to trust herself to Him every day. Brought up in a religious atmosphere deep in the Norfolk countryside, her father's ancient church close by and within sound and sight of the bells and tower of historic Lavenham, Trix developed and kept all her life a simple and unshaken trust in God and His love, a faith that was to be important to her in her work.

As a sturdy six- or seven-year-old there was nothing particularly pious about her behaviour, and she seems to have got into more scrapes than most. She it was who electrified the quiet village of Brent Eleigh in 1907 with the news that their Rector and his wife had been blessed by the arrival of a black son. Owing to the combination of an icy June and an attack of asthma young Master Havergal was the bluest of blue babies, with only a tenuous hold on life and requiring instant baptism from his alarmed father. Young Trix, primed with the usual doctor's bag delivery story, caught a glimpse of her mother nursing what was clearly a tiny black baby. In a trice she had found a postcard from her mother's desk, written in large letters, 'We have got a little black brother', addressed it to Frances and trotted with it to the village shop where, naturally, it became public property. The inhabitants of Brent Eleigh must have dined out on that startling information for days; meanwhile Christopher Havergal recovered magnificently, and these early glimpses of family life owe everything to his vivid memories and his Havergalian sense of atmosphere.

The education of the young Havergals was entrusted to a governess, the much loved Miss Holland or Honnie, and the two sisters took a very different view of proceedings in the schoolroom. Frances throve on academic work, Trix seems to have spent much valuable time in the corners, picking off the wallpaper as an outlet for her frustrated energies. Released after school hours she was off to much more exciting occupations, an unholy alliance with a gamekeeper's son, one Arthur Kewell, led to a totally forbidden assault on the roof of the church tower, involving a struggle with rotten ladders and slippery leads. On a less perilous but more significant level Trix set up her own carpenter's shop in a loose box in the stable. The usual basic tools were provided and the budding carpenter's first achievement was a proudly painted board announcing 'Odd Jobs Done Here'. Unfortunately for the young proprietor this was spotted by a young curate standing in for the Revd Clement who was away on Mission service and was improved, secretly, to 'Very Odd Jobs Done Here'. Another incident which, by contrast, may have boosted Trix's ego was a miscalculation by the elder, and seemingly infallible, Frances. Having read about parachutes she became convinced that flight from a ten foot high hayloft was entirely possible with the aid of an umbrella. For once Trix and the young Christopher doubted her wisdom and challenged her to give a demonstration. Heroically she did, landing safely but messily in a well-rotted dunghill, the effects of which could not be concealed from parents or governess.

A professional photograph taken in 1910 and in Christopher Havergal's possession shows the family in revealing poses. Frances at eleven is nestling against the long-skirted Miss Holland, Christopher, at three, is held tightly at his mother's knee. Trix stands sturdily on her own, boyishly cropped, wearing a smock-type dress over a strong pair of boots, and with a large turnip watch dangling round her neck from a piece of string. The Revd Clement is missing. From about this time the Havergal home, loving as it was, began to fall apart, a condition echoed on a gigantic scale by the outbreak of the First World War, which was to sweep away much that was familiar.

In 1912 the Havergal parents decided that the girls needed more discipline and a wider education, and the beloved Honnie, who must often have provided refuge from family squabbles, had to go. Frances was sent to a Boarding-School for Young Ladies in Kent, and was soon followed by Trix. The Headmistress rejoiced in the ominous name of Miss Bendall, but she was not destined to influence the Havergal girls for long. Shortly after war was declared increased tension in the Rectory led to a legal separation between Clement and his wife; the Rector was left to fend for himself at Brent Eleigh, and Mrs Havergal took the three children to a tiny house in Sidney Road, Bedford. The sisters could to go Bedford High School, good but inexpensive, and Christopher could begin at the Preparatory Department for Bedford School, known locally as the Incubator.

It was now that Trix became aware of a condition that was to dog her all her life, acute lack of money. The Havergals were very poor indeed; country parsons are seldom wealthy men and there were two households to maintain. By 1916 Mrs Havergal's health was causing anxiety; clearly savings had to be made, and she needed help at home. Her main assets were her daughters, so different in their physical and mental make-up. Frances, the industrious and academic, must stay at school, Trix, the energetic and apparently less gifted, must leave at fifteen, help her mother, and try to supplement the family finances. From now on she was free from comparison with her sister, and could develop her own rich talents. She immediately took on gardening jobs for friends in Bedford and became a member of the army of women land workers under the Women's County War Agricultural Committee, promising officially 'to work on the land whenever called upon to do so.'

One rather sad tale, often told by Beatrix Havergal herself, relates how one of her gardening jobs took her to a garden adjoining the Bedford High School playground, and how she used to dive into the tool shed at playtime to avoid the curiosity, and perhaps the taunts, of her former school friends. In 1917, war or no war, jobbing gardening would have seemed unusual and, to some, socially unacceptable for a clergyman's young daughter. Life cannot have been easy, but photographs of the period show signs of the Beatrix Havergal of the future, a robust, confident, and good-looking young woman, workmanlike in smock and breeches.

Before long things began to look up for the Havergals in general and for young Trix in particular. Her parents temporarily resolved their differences and Clement left Brent Eleigh to join his family in Bedford. This improved the financial situation; they were able to move to a better house in Chaucer Road, and there was a little money for a training for Trix. She had two options, a career in horticulture or one in music. She inherited much of the Havergal musical talent, had a strong and beautiful contralto voice, played the cello and was later able to coax sweet sounds out of an ancient church harmonium. The cost of a musical training, together with the uncertainty of success in such a competitive field, weighed against the music; it remained as a constant source of pleasure and relaxation instead. Horticulture offered a safer future, and Trix embarked on a two year course at the Thatcham Fruit and Flower Farm, near Newbury, Berks.

Chapter Two

Beatrix Havergal was to become a pioneer in the field of horticultural training for women and raise the standard of that training to great heights, but it must not be thought that she was first in the field. In 1895 the then Director of Kew Gardens experimented with female gardeners who, however, had to pick up knowledge as best they could. A wag observed that:

> From the tops of the buses they had a fine view
> of the ladies in bloomers who gardened at Kew.

More significantly women were admitted to Swanley College in 1900, and it became solely female in 1902. Studley in Warwickshire was founded in 1910 and survived until 1969, and Viscountess Wolseley had opened her School for Lady Gardeners at Glynde at the turn of the century. Indeed Frances Garnet Wolseley, down-to-earth, patriotic, class-conscious but far-seeing, was one of the first to realize that there was a real career for women in horticulture. She saw the necessity even then, of trying to halt the exodus from country to town, and was quick to see how society would be changed as a result of the 1914 war. In 1916 she wrote *In a College Garden*, a delightful account of the training at Glynde. Certain passages, allowing for differences of style, attitudes and general mores of her time, probably stir a few uncomfortable memories in former Waterperry students. Here she is writing on glasshouse work.

> So that students can be given absolute responsibility in ventilating glasshouses and watering plants the head organizer requires many qualities, in addition to the actual knowledge of growing plants. Patience is one of them. Through ignorance or carelessness crops suffer, and this is more often the case with work under glass than in outdoor gardening. How often in the early morning after the Captain has done her round of inspection do I hear the tolling of the great

> garden bell. I know then that some act of negligence has caused the death of one or more plants, and that the students are being summoned, not to a burial but to attendance, whilst reproof is being administered for this lack of care. The instant the first peal rings out, all drop their tools and hurriedly, breathlessly, come running up the hill to the students' office. If the offence is one of gross carelessness and means the loss of a considerable sum a fine is levied, and all subscribe to it. Perhaps freesia bulbs, placed on a warm shelf to get thoroughly dry have had water spilled on them by mistake and will consequently become rotten, or else melon plants that were to grow into finely developed bearers of good fruit have been allowed to get bone dry, so that Red Spider has shown itself on their leaves. All such acts of indifference or forgetfulness, where they affect the welfare of plants, must be punished, and the only thorough way of so doing is to make each member of the community feel individually affected by the mischief that has been done.

Strong words perhaps, but the writer met a Waterperry student who was unfortunate enough to break the top of her cucumber plant and who, forty years on, still considered it one of the most traumatic experiences of her life.

Glynde was clearly organized on 'all Sir Garnet' lines, and the same high standards must have been true of the Thatcham Fruit and Flower Farm School near Newbury. Here Miss Hughes-Jones and Miss Sowerby presided, working on similar lines to Glynde, and here the young Trix began a two-year course in 1917. This must have been one of the most carefree times in her life, learning her craft and finding where her real talents lay. Home problems, parent differences and lack of money did not just go away of course. Her parents separated again during her training, causing a new financial crisis, but Miss Hughes-Jones, with great generosity coupled with an eye for value, kept Trix on first without fees and then as a member of her staff. Mrs Havergal and Frances found a small flat in Hampstead where Trix and Christopher, now a boarder at Weymouth College, could join them for holidays. The Revd Clement eked out what must have been a rather dreary existence in 'digs'. The perpetual money shortage is well illustrated by a letter from Trix to her mother at some stage in her training. 'I went over to see a Miss Stewart about a room for next term. She has a dear little cottage just above the Head's, and she is Scotch and a lady. I would love to be there. I can't get anything at present under 5/- a week. Miss S. wants 5/-, but it is a nice big room — some of the others I can hardly turn round in. Do write and tell me if 5/- a week will be beyond our means.' Fortunately the 5/- was available, as a later letter speaks of Trix's box being moved to Miss Stewart's cottage.

Judging by lovingly preserved photographs Thatcham proved the ideal training ground for young Trix. Here she found order, craftsmanship, and knowledge, and she was ready to absorb all three. The system of French gardening, growing vegetables and salads under glass, was well in vogue, and as far back as 1909 the *Daily Mail* had reported an excellent exhibit of vegetables from Thatcham at a Show in Temple Gardens. A photograph of the French garden, sheltered with neat wattle fencing and showing row upon row of bell cloches all clearly marked Pilkington's British, every line regimented and measured together with perfectly aligned rows of frames, evokes a delightfully patterned and ordered atmosphere. Some very early photographs, probably taken soon after Thatcham opened, show the students in skirts to the ankle and long sleeved blouses, all covered with voluminous pinafores; piled up hair is much in evidence, crowned with the inevitable hat. Miss Hughes-Jones herself, a formidable person, is engaged in spraying a long bench of freesias with a very small brass syringe; her enormous hat-pin would seem to present an occupational hazard. Another splendid photo shows her driving the produce to market on a hard wheeled uncomfortable looking trolley, a spanking pony between the shafts; she has changed into a severe coat and skirt, of course with hat. By the time Trix joined the school the war situation had revolutionized the role of women, and the uniform had evolved to a rather shapeless button through smock over a long sleeved shirt with collar and tie, breeches, knee socks and strong shoes; the hats, still worn, were much reduced in size.

Trix's letters home, lovingly preserved by her mother, are ebullient and joyous, and full of her activities in everything but gardening. She had a new nickname, Gigs, for obvious reasons, and had made many friends equally ready to enjoy life. Summer seems to have been devoted to tennis — partners, opponents, and fiercely fought games take up most of the letters; the cost of a new white dress is cause for concern. She had joined the Thatcham Special Police Rifle Club and found that she was a very good shot; a souvenir of a record card, showing that she had scored 102 points out of a possible 105 at a Prize Shoot in 1919 remained a treasured possession. Music was a constant joy; she played her cello in the Newbury Orchestra and sang in the Choral Society, both requiring a good deal of bicycling, often with cello, and vast consumption of 'lardy cakes' at the Tudor Restaurant in Newbury.

But she was also — one might say at last — working with her head as well as her hands, needing both for her Preliminary Beekeeping examination in 1918. In 1920 she passed the Royal Horticultural Society's examination with First Class Honours, eighth in the year throughout the country. It is significant that in the 1920 list six women figure in the first ten, including the first and second, other colleges for women at that time including Huntsmoor Park, Iver, Aldersley Hall, Cheshire, Studley, Swanley in Kent and St James Gardens, Malvern. Trix was now ready for her first independent post.

A last letter from Lily Hughes-Jones speeds her on her way. 'My dear Gigs,' she writes, 'Our heartiest congratulations — we are simply delighted that you have done so well. Fancy being first of our folk — quite excellent. We are so pleased about you that we don't mind not having taken the medal. A fine send-off for you, coming the day you are going to your job. The results are very good all round — we have beaten Studley. We miss you very much. Much love from us both and the best of luck.'

Beatrix Havergal always intended to write her memoirs, and it was sad that when she finally retired she had neither the physical health nor the mental energy to do so, but she knew exactly where she would start, with a friendly "Hallo" over a hedge. Her first job was to prove a remarkable springboard for her career. Following Thatcham she contracted to design a new garden for a Mr and Mrs Atkinson who were building a bungalow in a field in the village of Cold Ash. The bungalow, Three Ways, was at the junction of three lanes, often used by walkers, and the young lady gardener would have been an object of interest to passers-by as she created her garden out of the raw field.

The most interested of the passers-by was Miss Olive Willis, founder and Head of Downe House School newly brought up from Kent and installed in buildings formerly used by an enclosed sisterhood. Olive Willis, unconventional educator of girls and always seeking ways of widening their horizons, was attracted by this energetic young gardener working single-handed and to her own design. Miss Willis also needed a gardener, and she was a very persuasive lady. Her walks past the Three Ways garden, usually accompanied by her friend and colleague Miss Heather and two Samoyed dogs, became a quest; gradually contact was made, and the, "Hallo — how are you getting on? When are you coming to see me?" a regular routine, tempered by the undeniable fact that Trix was contracted to Mrs Atkinson. But the move was inevitable, and when the designing and ground work at Three Ways was done and the garden could safely be left to another for the finishing touches Trix became Head Gardener at Downe House. It says much for Mrs Atkinson that she wrote a charming farewell letter, not a word of reproach but ending wistfully that 'it will be strange to look out on YOUR garden and see a man working.'

Olive Willis of the siren voice was to remain a tremendous influence in Beatrix Havergal's life, and the two women, pioneers in their own fields, had much in common. Trust, enthusiasm, and energy were three virtues amply displayed by both sides in their first agreement. Olive Willis had 300 acres for the school between Cold Ash and Hermitage, and she needed lawn tennis courts and gardens. The task facing Trix was to extend the existing garden and make six top quality grass courts out of established woodland. Trix's notes tell us much about both women. 'One felt one could not refuse her. A tall order for a nineteen-year-old and a woman at that. But the thrill of being entrusted with such an enterprise and the encouragement that Miss Willis gave me made it possible for me to overcome what at first seemed unsurmountable obstacles — a tree felling operation, the conversion of woodland and shingle soil to lawn grass, and the sheer magnitude of the task.' Years later in her retirement televised Wimbledon brought back memories of these Havergal courts at Downe House, and she wrote to her cousin Cynthia, 'I shall never forget the thrill of measuring up and marking out the three courts after mowing them; I would not allow anyone else to touch them.'

Her four years on Olive Willis's staff proved the turning point in Beatrix Havergal's life. She was a member of the staff common-room, one of a cultured and musical staff, and could admire at first hand Olive Willis's guidance of young people. Miss Willis disliked rigidity, used unconventional methods to discipline, and was unusually successful with unpromising material. She was also a woman of great warmth and affection, and a deeply committed Christian with a gift for presenting religion as an exciting adventure rather than as a matter of routine. She believed firmly that one could be endowed with Power from on High, and this looking to things of the Spirit perhaps had some bearing on her love of fresh air, as many former Downe House girls could testify. Beatrix Havergal entered into this little kingdom with great enthusiasm. Apart from her work she loved the evening services in Chapel when she would sit beside her friend Miss Heather and give a lead in singing 'seconds' in the hymns. Inspired by this atmosphere she began to dream of being able to pass on her own particular brand of knowledge, of owning her own horticultural school for women. By an incredible stroke of luck she was to meet a person at Downe who was to turn dreams into reality, her future partner Avice Sanders.

Avice Sanders had herself been a pupil at Downe House together with her two sisters; she had then trained in Domestic Science at Gloucester and she was back as Miss Willis's efficient housekeeper when the young lady gardener joined the staff. An instant rapport must have sprung up between the two women of similar backgrounds but of such differing personalities and temperaments. It is a curious fact that in later years few people in the horticultural world would have recognized or been able to name Beatrix Havergal's partner, yet theirs was to be a devoted, profitable, and equal partnership for more than forty years. A parallel that comes to mind is that of Sir Edward and Lady Elgar, the outgoing rumbustious genius, full of 'japes' and enthusiasms yet frequently in despair and doubtful of his own talent, and his quiet self-effacing wife who smoothed his path, restored his confidence, and dealt with the details of daily life. She quite literally ruled the paper on which his masterpieces were written. On a rather less exalted plane so it was with Beatrix Havergal and Avice Sanders. Throughout the years they spent together Avice provided the steady quiet background that her friend needed. Though little known she was no shadow; she was, in Beatrix's own words, 'a woman of great integrity, with initiative, courage and organizing ability,' her attitude to seemingly impossible enterprises simply, 'if you feel you want to do it, do it.'

As the friendship developed Beatrix confided in Avice her growing ambition to branch out, and to run her own horticultural school. Their joint assets were youth, energy and enthusiasm; financial assets were practically nil. The Sanders family was in rather better case than the Havergals, but they were not wealthy. However with immense courage, and about £250, the pair rented a small cottage and two acres of walled garden attached to the beautiful grounds of Pusey House, near Faringdon. To her eternal credit Olive Willis not only accepted with equanimity the loss of both gardener and excellent housekeeper but also whole-heartedly encouraged the pair with practical and moral support, and remained a staunch friend and counsellor all her life. Any furthering of opportunities for women was dear to her heart, and this venture by two of her protégées must have given her great satisfaction. September 1927 found the two established at Pusey and hoping for pupils. Two years earlier, in the neighbouring county of Oxfordshire a Miss Agnes Henley, last of her family to live in Waterperry House, had finally sold that house and estate to Magdalen College, Oxford, 2,900 acres in all including the surrounding woods. The square ivy-covered house had been a family home for centuries and was used to loving owners. For a few years it had to content itself with being an investment rather than a home; its future was to be even more exhilarating and its place in the annals of horticulture assured.

Chapter Three

Visitors to the lovely gardens surrounding Pusey House probably have no idea that they are stepping into horticultural history. Pusey, the former home of that family for generations, has plenty of history of its own. The founder of the family, Peisi, is alleged to have fought and spied for Canute, so successfully as to be rewarded with as much land as the sound of his horn could carry over. This ancient form of land tenure, called cornage, must have put good lungs and sharp ears at a premium. Closer to our own time the name of Pusey is an inseparable part of the great Oxford Movement in the Anglican Church. Its gardens with lawns leading to an expanse of water, brave borders and fine trees would seem the perfect setting for a horticultural college.

The Pusey acquired by Beatrix Havergal and Avice Sanders was rather different, and their 'dear dear Pusey' as Beatrix always described it, began on the wrong side of the main garden wall. In September, 1927, they rented the gardener's cottage from Philip Bouverie-Pusey, together with walled kitchen garden and glasshouses, and the Pusey Fruit and Flower Gardens were born. The main object was to attract students, and the printed prospectus reads well. 'The training will consist of a Theoretical and thoroughly Practical Training in the various branches of Horticulture, including soils and manures, glasshouse management, pruning and garden construction. Complete courses of lectures will be given, and students may enter for the Royal Horticultural Society's examinations if desired. Cookery classes can be taken during the two winter terms for an extra fee of £3.3.0 per term. Jam Making and Fruit Bottling a speciality. The Students will reside at the house in the garden and will each have a separate bedroom. Fees, inclusive of board, residence and tuition for the full two year course will be £95 per annum.' It all seems a tall order for a staff of two living in fairly primitive conditions.

While waiting for their students to appear Beatrix and Avice had a great deal to do. The walled garden had been run as a market garden by one Grimmett, but it had been allowed to fall into disrepair and disorder, its traditional box hedges nearly meeting across its paths. One romantic looking corner was so thick with ferns and weeds that they totally concealed a well — into which Beatrix duly fell. Luckily it was not too deep and the ferns proved strong enough to haul on. Despite the neglect the garden had great romantic charm with its Cotswold stone walls topped with pink valerian in summer, the established apple and pear trees trained on the walls, the stone archways dividing the whole into three divisions or slips. One of the three, running along the north side and shaded by beech trees in the main gardens, is now used as the selling area for present-day visitors to buy plants. The glasshouses consisted of two vineries and two plant houses.

Clearly it was not enough for the two friends in their straitened circumstances just to tidy their garden and wait for someone to turn up. The wall fruit provided the first possible asset, and they began to deliver fresh fruit and vegetables to Oxford dons and other worthies, using Avice's Austin Seven. They had good contacts in the area and began to get known; their first regular Oxford order was to supply an undergraduate with fresh fruit at his College, his mother obviously mistrustful of the effects of dining in Hall. His sister, a former pupil at Downe House, was to be a staunch friend and benefactress all their lives. The Austin Seven was soon insufficient for their needs, and Olive Willis's support took concrete form in the gift of an old T-model Ford tourer which they were able to convert into a van. They were now able to take a stall in Swindon Market on Saturdays where they hoped to sell surplus produce. As newcomers, and not the usual stall-holding types, they were regarded with suspicion at first and were none too busy, so used the spare time by pricking out bedding plants, taking in prepared boxes of soil and the seedlings for that purpose. The quality of the plants was evident and soon appealed to the many gardeners among the railway workers of Swindon; a regular income, though small, was assured. During this time Avice worked beside her partner in the gardens and at the stall, looked after hens and reared chicks as well as doing the housekeeping at the cottage.

The great breakthrough for the pair came quite dramatically with a call from the Carlton Hotel, London — "I understand you have a Training College for women." The gardener's cottage may have had delightful surroundings but it was hardly luxurious. Upstairs it boasted three bedrooms, but one had been partitioned to make two tiny rooms and leave space on the landing for a hip bath. Downstairs there were another three rooms and a kitchen, but the designated Students' common-room was a mere passage room between sitting-room and kitchen.

There was no water laid on, hence the hip bath, but it was obtained from the pump in the garden, and there was the usual earth closet outside. An ancient relic of a boiler, requiring much raking out and stoking, lurked in the basement of the building and provided necessary warmth in winter. A far cry from the Carlton Hotel but, none the less, a Training College in waiting. The caller from London was a Professor Reinhart, a wealthy Swiss academic, seeking a horticultural training for his daughter, Annelise. The telephone call must have been satisfactory as not long after a chauffeur-driven Rolls-Royce arrived at the gate of Pusey House itself. What Professor Reinhart thought on being redirected to the cottage tucked away in the house's shadow is not recorded, but, clearly, he was much impressed with what he found there; the enthusiasm, energy and sheer faith of the enterprise must have appealed to him, together with the sterling worth of the young principals themselves. Hard-headed Professors are seldom given to prophecy, but prophesy he did. His parting words were, "I see you in a large rectangular country house among trees, Miss Havergal. Look for it." Such a building must have seemed an impossible dream at that juncture. However in the autumn of 1928 Annelise Reinhart from Switzerland and Diana Purcell, a seventeen-year-old whose parents were in India, became the first Pusey students.

By great good fortune Annelise's mother preserved all her letters home, and they provide an authentic record and vivid picture of the Pusey days. Much later Annelise Burchhardt-Reinhart copied the initial three back for Miss Havergal's own records, and the foreign phrasing adds to their charm.

September 19th, 1928.

At last I am alone in my own room, which is a very sweet bedroom. Though it is facing north and has very little sun I do appreciate the view into the beech trees. I have already put photographs on the mantelpiece which can be looked at from my bed. The curtains are of bright colours — the wash-stand is white with an old jug and wash-basin glazed inside, earthenware. On the lower board of that wash-stand an object is turned upside down, which Diana (the other student) calls 'the Jeremiah'. Further a table, a chair, a chest. We are but two students here. Diana Purcell is a girl of seventeen from Sussex. Her parents live out in India. She wants to stay here for two years and take her final examination to be a teacher in horticulture. She has her room next to mine.

I studied my timetable. Work begins at seven o'clock. I shall get up at a quarter past six. This is very early for a lazy person like me, who wants to sit up late and write letters or read. We have breakfast at eight. Miss Havergal said we need not begin at seven tomorrow morning. After breakfast we have to make our beds and tidy up our rooms. We start our first job in the garden at nine o'clock. Lunch is at one o'clock. After lunch we have written lectures, every day except on Thursdays and Saturdays. After lectures we again go out in the garden, until tea-time at five. After tea we are free to do what we like until half-past seven when we have supper. After tea a lady came round to ask for three pounds of beans. Miss Havergal and Miss Sanders were rather upset to have to rush out again to see whether there were beans or not. Diana and I asked if we should go and see. So the two dear ladies took us round and in no time the beans were picked. After this Miss Sanders took me out in her Austin Seven to Faringdon where she sold two bags of plums.

My first day here did not seem to have been a long one. We had a nice long supper and it was very comfortable to sit and talk, the four of us, while Miss Havergal's Sealyham dog Jim and Miss Sanders' dog Beau rush round after the stone-deaf white cat called Fluff. Beau is friendly and rubs his head on my knees under the table. Miss Sanders got up and went into the kitchen. Fluff quickly hopped on the empty chair to look in Miss Sanders' plate and smell the end of her fork, shutting both eyes as if to forget what was smelling so good.

My English is still bad. I cannot find my words quickly so nobody takes the trouble to wait until I stammer an answer, if I am asked. Diana promised to correct my errors.

The young maid with the name of Alice takes care of our rooms. She brings us a jug of warm water every morning and every evening. She is only 14 years old, and is Miss Sanders' first pupil. She learns housework and cooking for us. By the way, I am afraid so, I begin to like gardening and maybe I will stay here and work for the R.H. Diploma.

September 30th, 1928.

My dear sister,

I am sorry that you never came to England with me. Pusey is such an interesting place, and the two ladies who run this school are very kind. This morning I went to church with Miss Havergal and Miss Sanders, before breakfast. We came back at nine. When we entered

Chapel the parson was standing by the altar. He was dressed very like a Roman Catholic priest. His name is Mr Norris. He is liked in this village by doing a lot of good for the people. Pusey estate exists since 1014 and was given to Pusey by Canute. In those days written documents did not exist. So a beautiful horn was given to the knight Pusey, adorned with gold, and in beautiful writing the king's will was expressed, that this estate should remain in Pusey's hands and that these 4,000 acres could not be taken from him ever. It is now over 900 years since. The peasants here have no land of their own — they have to rent it. Miss Havergal has rented the kitchen gardens of the estate and could not buy them if she wants to.

Last Friday was my marketing day. It was great fun. We took a lot of fruit, vegetables and flowers, all nicely done up, to Oxford. It was raining, we were glad to sit in the little Ford van. We took a crate of pears each to a fruit stall. Miss Havergal asked the man, "Would you want these pears?" He wanted them. We brought him about 60 pounds of them. Then we went to a flower stall, she bought a box full of asters. After that we went to the back door of three customers. Miss Havergal made a remark about feeling funny to have to use the back door. I did not mind a bit — but after all she is a parson's daughter and has not been used to selling stuff at back doors. Nevertheless people seem to get to know Pusey Gardens and ask for a selection of vegetables. It is sometimes difficult to get two pounds of beans, carrots, beetroot and four pounds of tomatoes four times over. One customer brought her five others and now Miss Havergal says "I really don't know where this will end." People are very polite. When Miss Havergal comes round to the fruit store kept by Mr Smart, a stout man, she asks, "Could you do with these pears this week?" "Oh, certainly, Madam," says the man with beaming face. Then Miss Havergal takes her book out and writes at the bottom of the page: Received with thanks, B. Havergal. I was sorry to see that our beautiful violet bunches have been sold 3d each. The flower stall keeper was so eager to have them that she would gladly have given more. Everything is done up so nicely in Pusey Gardens that people just can't resist buying.

After my first week here, looking at my diary I feel that I learnt quite a few things. Our first job was brushing pots with a steel brush to make them ready for potting early strawberries. We had to prepare crocks, put them over the hole in the pot, then a layer of straw over them. Miss Havergal showed us how to mix soil. Then we potted the maiden strawberry plants: 130 King George, 50 The Duke, and only 20 Royal Sovereign. In the afternoon we picked apples and pears. Bunching asters was a nice job, flat bouquets of twelve flowers ready to be packed in boxes for the market next day. Every single job seemed to be an interesting one. We went out to collect leaf mould in the woods. We dug up the tomato plants in the glasshouse preparing it for the pots of arum lilies, tulips to be grown in this house for forcing in the spring. We potted Roman hyacinths, narcissus, and tulips. My first Saturday was a gay one, after having done some cleaning of the marketing shed, storing some apples, clearing two frames and putting the straw away in the pot and box house Miss Havergal announced that we were going out tonight, because she and Miss Sanders were now here for a whole year today. We went to the cinema to see 'The Stolen Bride'.

September, 1928.

Dear Marilese,

Thank you for your letter from Brienz. I pity you that you are not allowed to go out on a Sunday. You are not even going to church. Perhaps you would not even like it there but here Diana and I like Service very much. Please tell our parents that Mother should not always write letters to Miss Havergal about what I should do here. Father thinks that he wants me to practise the violin and he will write about it, I do not miss music here. I do not want to practise and I prefer to learn my lectures instead. It would make a bad impression and again Miss Sanders and Miss Havergal would notice that I am a spoilt girl who tries to have this, that, and the another.

I still hate to get up in a hurry. When it is dark and grey outside I comfort myself by picturing the nice bowl of porridge and cream which I get for breakfast at eight — so that helps a bit. Food is very good. We get a real English breakfast. After porridge there would be either fish, bloaters, or sausages or ham with eggs — then tea, bread and butter with orange marmalade. On Sundays we open up the glasshouses, the frames, etc. Then Diana takes me to church. After church we do a bit of watering in the glasshouses then we have lunch. It consists of a big joint of beef, potatoes and a vegetable, for instance sprouts or onions. After the main course there is a pie — apples with raisins in a stew-pan covered with pastry. I like this dish very much. During the afternoon hours we read or listen to the radio. We shall hear the Lehner Quartet too.

I forgot to tell you that on Saturdays we go to Swindon market to sell the products from our gardens. Last Saturday I went to Swindon with Miss Havergal in the morning taking our sandwiches along with hot tea in a thermos. The market hall is not as nice as the one in Oxford. Swindon is very much like Toss near Winterthur. The population to buy in the market is mainly from the hardworking class and not wealthy. We sell flowers and rooted cuttings, seedlings in boxes for flower beds, and fruit. Miss Havergal has a stall there. It consists of a big table. At both ends of it we put the tins with the cut flowers. In the centre we have the seed-boxes with forget-me-nots, sweet-williams, pansies and primulas. It is a lovely show, especially at the beginning, when the rush has not started.

I had to go to town to try to get a hat for my uniform. Miss Havergal came with me to buy new shoes, while Miss Sanders came with Diana to see us off and take care of the stall in the meantime. It was very difficult to find suitable shoes. Shoes for ladies were too expensive and none had flat heels with broad soles. I had to try the smallest boys' shoes. Miss Havergal laughed and said these were now real beetle-crushers. I must also have a new mackintosh. I am small and stout so it has been ordered to fit me. I hoped very much that I should be able to sell some more at the stall but Diana would not let me. So I went home with Miss Sanders while Miss Havergal stayed on until nine. I was going to shut down the glasshouses. But oh the key to the door of the walled-in gardens was in Swindon in Miss Havergal's pocket. It was getting cold and we expected frost for the night. I got the ladder out of the marketing shed, climbed up on the wall with the kerosene lamp, drew the ladder up and down the other side, and did the work that had to be done. It was nine when I finished, covering the violets with hessian. We began to eat dinner at half-past nine, while Miss Havergal and Diana were on their way home. We had a long long dinner, mashed potatoes with minced meat, a little cup of broth — then tea with bread and butter and treacle. Miss Havergal was pleased to bring back the cash-box with £4/19/3. I felt like buying something for ninepence to make it even to five pounds. What a shame that I could not.

I hope that you will send me your timetable. I would like to know what you are doing in your school. It must be very different from this place here. The nice part about Pusey gardens is, that we work all day with our teacher, who keeps explaining all the time, how and why things should be done that way and not another.

> Next Sunday we will probably go to Newbury with Miss Sanders and Miss Havergal.

When Annelise Burchhardt-Reinhart gave the writer permission to use her letters in this history she added another amusing anecdote that she remembered from her Pusey days. Again it is recorded in her own words, sounding very much like the enthusiastic if anxious student of earlier years.

> Another funny experience was that we had twice punctured tyres on the van which we used for going to Swindon market. It was dark and as late as nine o'clock p.m. when we came home in that car. Miss Havergal drove. I was sitting beside her and held the cash-box on my knees. Now, after the tyre went flat we stepped out and had to help each other mending the tyre on the roadside. It took quite a long while. We crept into the van again and drove home, very tired of course. I think it was over 10 p.m. by then. We had a nice dinner and as we chatted about the good amount of money we got for the flowers and fruit Miss Havergal suddenly cried out, "Oh Annelise, where's the cash-box?" While she asked I got so frightened I could hardly get up from my seat, remembering that during the mending of the tyre I had placed the cash-box on the front mudguard and never remembered to have taken it back into the car. So I rushed out and said, "I know where it is" — Miss Sanders at once after me with suspicious looks. In the dark garage I got round the van and opened the door, that Avice should think that I had left it in the car — but it was still sitting on the mudguard. I could not believe it and was so relieved. Of course I never told anybody about it, you are the first one to know.

The early Pusey days do seem to have been rather special, every one bringing a new discovery for Annelise, and spent in an unaffected happy atmosphere where small triumphs brought real pleasure. When, for example, Annelise was on holiday in London in 1929 she had a joyous letter from Beatrix Havergal dated 18th April telling her that the Pusey glasshouse strawberries were the first anywhere that year. No one else could advertise any, and there were none even in London, while Miss Havergal had sold two pounds for twenty-four shillings, a vast sum.

The two ladies had already taken on two men to help them get the garden in trim, two very different characters who were eventually to become part of the Waterperry staff. The first, Fred Whitting, was a cheerful friendly cock-sparrow of a man, who had served in the cavalry in World War One, losing part of his hand in action though fortunately not his fingers. He had tried working for a local builder, then turned to gardening as a kinder option. His wife was a clever dressmaker and had many clients in Faringdon, so Fred had a daily trip of six miles or so to work. He retained his cavalry air, neat in breeches and leggings and homburg hat, topped while at work with a green baize apron, and 7 a.m. found him in his little shed, polishing the ladies' shoes until they shone like conkers, accompanying himself with his own Pooh Bear type of song — or noise — a 'tiddeley-pom' of his own invention. At first he knew nothing of gardening but did the basic jobs such as pot washing and soil mixing, gradually making himself indispensable. One of his pet phrases ran, "Six days shall thou labour, and the seventh day do all the odd jobs," and it suited him, always busy and enthusiastic. The second worker, John Hogarth, was, and remained, a mystery man. He seems literally to have come round the corner with a horse and cartload of coal and stayed, presumably having first returned the horse, proving to be both knowledgeable and skilled in horticulture. He had apparently worked in a nursery near Edinburgh, but that was all that ever emerged; he had no family and no background that he cared to divulge, and when probed in later years he would smile gently and make great play with lighting his pipe, so preventing further conversation. He was scruffy in appearance and frequently sarcastic about Fred Whitting's sartorial splendour, yet he was quiet and cultivated in his speech. Even his landlady, curious like all landladies about her lodger, learnt no secrets, and could only report that Mr Hogarth took in very 'highbrow' magazines.

In December, 1930, this activity led to a great step forward, the appointment of the first trained woman to be a member of the staff. Peggy Chaplin, now Mrs Peggy Fonge and to whom these chapters are deeply indebted, had trained at Reading University, and had been working at Clarence Elliott's famous nursery. Miss Havergal's letter to her in November stated that she was anxious to find someone to help work up the garden as a business concern and especially to take over the task of building up a stock of perennials and provide cut flowers. Expansion was in the air; they had acquired two acres of open allotment for fruit and vegetables and students were now coming. One of the newcomers, Mary Rowlatt, quickly fell under the spell. She wrote, 'I arrived in 1929, aged twenty-one, with a one-sided experience of life and not having worked with my hands. The green uniform took my fancy exceedingly, and I had perked it out with an expensive red silk spotted handkerchief and tie to match. On my tongue was a string of exotic botanical names alluding to our sub-tropical garden in Egypt, having no relevance to the work in hand. But under all this I really did want to learn and do my best, so the sensible spirit of Pusey soon took over. As for the cottage and all its subsidiaries, pump water and earth closet, it opened up new and excitingly genuine aspects of life. The whole thing seemed most delightful and stimulating.' Diana Purcell left that year but Annelise stayed until 1930 and left triumphantly with a first-class RHS certificate and the status of a legend. When Peggy Chaplin joined the staff they had three other students and had rented a second cottage in the village. Finally they rented The Croft, a delightful cottage owned by the Puseys and just five minutes from the gardens, and Peggy, with three students, moved in there. To her relief this afforded much more privacy and, joy of joys, the hip bath could be used in front of the kitchen fire.

There were set-backs of course. In the autumn of 1929 Beatrix went on a trip to Italy as chauffeur to Miss Willis and Miss Heather, rashly drank untreated water in spite of warnings and went down with a severe dose of typhoid. It was nearly six months before she was fit again, and the situation was only saved by Miss Willis who sent Beatrix's successor at Downe House to run the Pusey gardens. Money was desperately tight and they now had two men and a trained woman on the payroll. This might not seem too burdensome when we learn that Peggy Chaplin, a graduate, earned her keep and £1 per week, 1/6 of which had to go in National Insurance. On the other hand low prices meant that little came in. The Pusey catalogue of 1931 lists bedding plants at 6d and 8d a dozen, pot geranium Paul Crampel at 7d each, with brassica plants at 1/6 per hundred. The industry shown by everyone was incredible and they worked all hours. Avice Sanders was by now fully occupied on the domestic side, catering simply but superbly on a tiny budget, supportive and encouraging. Beatrix Havergal worked with her students by day and on her own lectures and her study for the National Diploma by night. Peggy Chaplin thought it not unusual to be bunching flowers for market at two in the morning. One evening only was set aside for recreation; on Mondays Beatrix would go into Oxford and Bach Choir practices, and occasionally the others would go in with her and go to the pictures. Sunday was always kept as the Sabbath. Essential watering and ventilating, no more, and church-going took up the morning, and the two Principals often spent the rest of the day at Downe House. To Peggy Chaplin, used to livelier society, it was incredibly quiet, transport was by bicycle only and the alternative occupations were walking or working, usually the latter.

Regarding the students' training it was clear that Beatrix Havergal started on the level at which she intended to stay, at the top. Miss Howard-Jones and Miss Willis had shown her high standards of efficiency and inspirational teaching, and the Pusey girls received great care. Student and teacher worked side by side, wearing the identical uniform that was to become Miss Havergal's trade mark, green breeches with green knee stockings, masculine type shirts buttoned to the neck with a tie, a green smock overall for good measure and, always, a hat. Every detail of training was considered, the meticulous care and use of tools, the preparation of fruit and vegetables for market, how to produce quality backed by presentation. The students themselves received the same attention and affection. Mary Rowlatt wrote about a picnic on the downs. 'It happened to be my birthday but I don't remember having mentioned the fact. We all enjoyed it, but when the time came for the tea, to my total surprise a magnificent birthday cake complete with candles was unpacked and even lighted in the teeth of the downland wind.'

1931 found Pusey Fruit and Flower Gardens in good heart, gaining in reputation and building up a goodly range of herbaceous plants among other stock. It was clearly the time to expand, to go out and look for Professor Reinhart's country house among trees. One can imagine the discussions going on late at night between the two friends, Beatrix voluble, gesticulating, seeing visions yet hesitant, Avice the quietly disciplined 'talking post' making the decisions, two women of immense courage and faith. One or two possible places were visited and rejected; legend has it that Avice would monopolize the owner by discussing domestic details at length while Beatrix hastily dug up soil samples from outside. Then in the same year Magdalen College, Oxford, were looking for new tenants to rent Waterperry House near Wheatley; here at last was the country house of their dreams.

Chapter Four

Miss Havergal's diary for 31st August, 1932, reads 'Moved to Waterperry from Pusey, dear Pusey. What a step — what a contrast.' Certainly Waterperry House seemed the perfect fulfilment of Professor Reinhart's prophecy, standing four-square in parkland, looking over an expanse of flat fertile Oxfordshire soil. But with their slender resources could they manage it? Their assets, as always, were mainly based on human endeavour. Apart from the partners themselves the pioneers were the invaluable Peggy Chaplin, six students of whom one was learning domestic subjects, the faithful Whitting, the enigmatic Hogarth, and James, the Sealyham dog.

The outgoing tenant was Mrs O'Connor, mother of Sir Richard, one of our finest generals in the war to come. The legend on her simple memorial in Waterperry church endears her to the village for all time — 'Lily O'Connor, who lived at Waterperry and loved it'. Peggy Chaplin remembered her clearly as a tiny lady opening the big front door of the house just enough to peep round it when they first visited the estate. It was a huge house for one small lady, even with servants, and she chose to sleep in a large four-poster bed in one corner of the ballroom with a pipe organ for company, while her small dog cocked his leg round the room with impunity and discoloured the curtains. But she was a practical person in all other respects and was to be most helpful to the in-comers.

Lily O'Connor loved her garden, and must have been glad that it was to pass into such caring hands, even if it had to be aroused from slumber. Its focal point was the walled garden, then full of mature fruit trees, fruit trained on the walls and in a fruit cage, with borders of flowers for cutting. Beyond the wall was the herbaceous border, already fine but to be considerably widened later, a good collection of peonies flourishing at the far end of the lawn, while an enormous hedge of unpruned rambler roses blocked the way to the field below, adding to the Sleeping Beauty effect. The Pusey party fell in love with it all, and Miss Havergal was fascinated by the orange tree growing in the conservatory, as visitors are fascinated today. She took one orange back to Pusey, its scent and strangeness so evocative of the vast garden and its possibilities; perhaps it helped in the final brave decision.

Obviously the move did not happen overnight, and 1931 had its sorrows and triumphs for Pusey. Mrs Havergal died very suddenly from influenza, and Trix had adored her mother, but this had not prevented her from passing her National Diploma in Horticulture, the highest award available for a practical gardener. Her final practical tests took place at Wisley in June of the following year, and the result arrived at Pusey just before the move. The work at Pusey had gone on regardless of impending change; every penny was needed and crops were there to be harvested, grapes from the vinery, tomatoes from the orange boxes on the staging steps, flowers and fruit to go to market. There can never have been enough hours in the day. That spring they had brought out a splendidly comprehensive catalogue of bedding plants; these would have been disposed of by midsummer, but the stock herbaceous plants had to be tended. There were more domestic details to cope with thinking of the future. Mrs O'Connor offered advice about cows; her Waterperry cows had brought in £165-19-7 in cash besides all the milk, cream and butter for the house, but there were expenses. "If you have no experience of cows I should advise you not to start them at first, even although they are profitable. How impertinent of me to advise you." They took her advice gratefully. They now had a mansion to care for and to heat, and one can only smile wryly at the list of coal prices sent to B. Havergal, Esq: from the Coal Exchange, London. It offered Good Small Furnace Coke for 28 Shillings and 6 Pence a ton, Coke Nuts for 30 Shillings and Best House Coal for 31, all delivered free of charge to Wheatley Station. Jottings on the list indicate that they settled for thirty-five tons of Coke.

Other investments had to be made for the new conditions, and they bought a 14 cwt. Ford van, and spent all of £8 on a table. Miss Havergal went to a sale with the intention of buying a cart; she got carried away and bought three, so one horse had to go backwards and forwards collecting them. At last the final details were completed with Magdalen College; the lease, dated 26th August 1932, was for twenty-one years on a rising rent, £150 for the first three years, £200 for the fourth and fifth, rising to £300; they were being given a chance to prove themselves.

The students were on holiday in August, so it was a tiny band involved on the 31st of that month. Miss Sanders and a friend, Miss Gage, later to become headmistress of Headington School, went ahead, Miss Havergal and Peggy Chaplin following in the Austin Seven which was bursting with precious or overlooked items; the dog James was on Peggy's lap and the clock lodged under her knees. The furniture removal men unloaded the contents of Pusey into the entrance hall of Waterperry House and probably grinned to themselves as they drove away. They were not the only ones to express doubt. Miss Sanders's lawyer uncle had previously surveyed the hall from the wide staircase and said, "You two girls have a nerve taking on a place like this." The bleak effect was softened a little by the fact that Mrs O'Connor left many of the carpets, and some fine pieces of furniture including four-poster beds and a pair of tallboys. But it was a very big change from the gardener's cottage. At supper that night they celebrated with a bottle of wine that Avice Sanders had found in the capacious cellars, and drank to the future while sitting round the kitchen table; typically Avice was worried that Munday, who had been Mrs O'Connor's chauffeur and whom they were taking on, should see them actually eating in the kitchen. One can only guess at the feelings of the two friends as, on the following morning, they looked out on their new estate with all its problems and possibilities.

For a short time they shuttled between Waterperry and Pusey making the final adjustments. The last Pusey produce had to be marketed, and many of the plants could not be lifted and moved until October. There were all the winter chrysanthemum to come, every root wrapped in sacking, in order to be planted in the Waterperry glasshouses, a task that worried Fred Whitting to distraction for weeks before. At last the move was complete and all energies could be concentrated on Waterperry. The students settled in after their vacation, rattling a little in the great cold house that first winter. Three of them should have left after Pusey but stayed on for a year to help out, getting only their keep, an arrangement that speaks volumes for both parties. Fred Whitting and his wife found a council house in Waterperry village, and the inscrutable Hogarth found another landlady.

In those early days they must all have felt rather like A. A. Milne's shipwrecked sailor who could not decide what to do first. But the house itself with its air of graciousness and serenity, and the marvellous small church only separated from it by the width of the churchyard, provided a unique setting for their new lives. The church was central both in its position and to their own convictions, and they immediately began the practice of meeting for prayers every working morning. Avice Sanders, who would have loved to have been there, was, characteristically, cooking breakfast, Martha-like. Beatrix Havergal played the harmonium for a hymn, strode up to the reading desk to read a biblical passage and lead prayers. This short totally sincere dedication of both workers and work each morning made a great impression on many of the students through the years. Of course some were indifferent, and a few brave unbelievers cut it; in the latter years a more cynical generation mainly opted out. But the writer was given a vivid picture by one of the earliest students of the quiet church, and the rows of identical brown felt hats just visible in the deep box pews as their wearers prayed together.

Those felt hats could be said to embody much of the atmosphere of pre-war Waterperry; they were durable and workmanlike, they were, above all, ladylike. It is no secret that the Principals looked for students from upper class origins; they intended to turn out lady gardeners or lady teachers of gardening, keeping the most talented of them as junior staff for a year or two. They also needed fees desperately. Consequently the first intakes were somewhat mixed in motive; a proportion certainly came to be 'finished', or to kill time before 'coming out'. No academic standard was needed, and one or two older women came to recover from broken marriages, tough therapy indeed. This sort came and went, no doubt benefiting from the experience, but the true pioneers of those early days, the 'stalwarts' to use Miss Havergal's phrase, were giants. Not necessarily physically — in the autumn of 1934 a tiny girl with a severe spinal curvature and a beautiful face arrived for interview from Owestry High School, recommended by a teacher who had formerly taught Botany to the girls at Pusey. Miss Havergal looked down at her from her considerable height, and wondered how she could accept such a frail creature, but Joan Stokes's confident and delightful smile settled the issue. She was accepted and played a vital role in the school's development, superbly competent in the glass department and responsible for the display of strawberries at Chelsea year after year.

This hard-working but essentially country house atmosphere remained until the outbreak of war. The students were cared for absolutely, waited on at table, perhaps asked to make their own beds but no more. The food was excellent, simple but beautifully cooked, there were log fires in the common-rooms but freezing bedrooms in winter — the house had its own electricity supply while the village had none. Every Saturday night full length dresses were *de rigueur*, Miss Havergal remembered as looking handsome in green velvet but almost undressed without collar and tie. All the ladies gathered in the drawing-room after dinner and there might be music, perhaps gramophone records, or Miss Havergal might be persuaded to sing. Students were, in theory, permitted to go out, but were not really expected to use the permission; men were treated with the utmost suspicion, a Victorian attitude which persisted even into the seventies, and which ingenious students down the decades managed to circumvent. The doors were locked at a very early hour. One Kitty Swanwick, who had acquired both a sports car and a fiancé in 1933, found herself locked out one evening and whistled up to Peggy Chaplin's window for assistance. Peggy, tiptoeing downstairs, saw Avice Sanders in front of her and strategically retreated. Avice, in the half-dark, opened the outside door to be slapped on the back by Kitty and told that she was a real sport. History does not relate her response, but those who were much in awe of Avice Sanders will enjoy the tale.

None of these social niceties were allowed to deflect the Principals from their goal however, and all their energies were devoted to one end, to provide the best horticultural training in the country. Social standing may have been hoped for in students but neither Principal had time or inclination for social life as such. The local gentry called and left the right number of cards with due regard for etiquette, such as the Tyndale-Biscoes of Holton Park and the formidable Miss Ashhurst, last of a long line, from the other side of the river in Waterstock. If they caught sight of one of the new tenants they may have been surprised by the breeches and smock attire. Only the Bach Choir remained for recreation for Miss Havergal; both worked into the night, and the students were usually too tired at the end of the day to do more than write up their diaries and work notes and fall into bed. In the longer summer days they played tennis on the patched-up court in front of the house, the Principals very properly dressed in long sleeved white dresses and stockings, with summer hats; otherwise decorous picnics and trips on the little River Thame in the rowing boat, Piglet, were the main highlights of the year. They soon established a tradition of celebrating Miss Havergal's birthday in July — characteristically Miss Sanders kept her January birthday very quietly — and usually had a picnic on a grand scale. In 1938 for example they all repaired to the White Horse hill at Uffington, the indefatigable Miss Sanders providing a splendid supper again completed with cake and candles, and they stayed until the glow-worms came out on the ancient hill.

Meanwhile the gardens were being tamed and developed to provide the outdoor class-room that was needed. The training called for experience in as many different branches of horticulture as possible, and the teaching aspect was considered first in any planning. However some private ambitions began to be realized. Peggy Chaplin had always hoped to build up an Alpine nursery and here she had opportunity, free from interference from Miss Havergal who always preferred the grand strategy to the actual plants. Given a free hand, though doubtless no more time, Peggy was able to exhibit saxifrages at one of the Royal Horticultural Society's fortnightly Shows as early as 1935, so laying the foundation for the fine collection of kabschias, later developed by Valerie Finnis, and still the most comprehensive in the country. Miss Havergal, with eyes on the broader acres was longing to plant fruit in the rough field south of the garden, then gated at each end and fenced off. With Peggy's help she strode it out and measured up by the light of the moon one frosty night, and the line of apple cordons came into being. All cultivation was by hand, and the entire south field was eventually dug with spades; they owned one motor mower for the formal lawns, and the broad grass paths elsewhere were scythed by Reuben Clifford, another man taken on the staff but not allowed to work near the students because of his language.

Gradually many of the old trees in the kitchen garden were cleared, the fruit cage demolished as other fruit became available and the area took on an air of orderliness and efficiency. Betty Thin, one of the first 'stalwarts' cut down two large elms single-handed from behind the churchyard wall, removed them together with a formidable rubbish dump, and built the Alpine rock garden in their place. Another rock garden was started beyond the little bridge at the end of the lawn, only to be abandoned at the outbreak of war. Neat lines of frames now stood in front of the three glasshouses; it was discovered that Mrs O'Connor's gardener had managed to dispose of the manure from six cows almost exclusively in this area with remarkable results. The green and black vines in the house adjoining the conservatory with its orange tree were a constant worry for more anxious students, since one hair touching the fruit was deemed to have spoilt the bloom. There were hens, there were bees, there were the fearsome boilers which emanated a remarkable fall-out of pink dust and which required stoking; they were all very hard-worked, very conscientious and in most cases very happy. The pitch in Swindon was kept on, and every Friday Miss Havergal and two students took in produce, a real outing and very popular. It could be quite eventful. On one trip Betty Thin called Miss Havergal's attention to a wheel rolling along beside the van; rather too late they realized it was their own, Ruth du Bois was on the homeward journey one day when they passed a fair; the old Charlie Trix asserted herself and they spent a riotous hour or so on the swings, presumably on the proceeds of the produce.

How — or why perhaps — did they do it all? The answer certainly lies in the person of Beatrix Havergal herself and the infection of enthusiasm. Like her mentor Olive Willis before her, you could not refuse her. The personal approach never failed; "How splendid you are — what should we do without you?" meant that all were determined to be more splendid still. She could be both unjust and narrow minded, she lacked Olive Willis's understanding of young people, and she constantly angled for reassurance and compliments. "Trix needs a lot of butter," Avice told Peggy in an unguarded moment. But she was a craftsman and a teacher *par excellence*, and a leader who led from the front and never spared herself.

These attributes, which invariably meant much time spent out of doors, was perhaps not always appreciated by the landlords, Magdalen College. Beatrix Havergal was never an efficient desk woman; that particular piece of furniture was always piled high with papers that had been put on one side, and her 'In' tray, had she owned one, would seldom have been countered by her 'Out' She had, during her time at Waterperry, two most admirable and efficient secretaries in Hilda Johns and, later, Margery Coe, who could have dealt with any problems in their stride if allowed to do so, but she was unwilling to dictate letters and would not delegate. Her letters always had a very personal touch and were an expression of her ebullient self, and this made dictation difficult. But there was no excuse for the frequent dash into the lavatory after tea, armed with the daily paper, so as to avoid Hilda Johns' attempts to finish the day's correspondence.

On all counts Magdalen College, through successive Bursars, emerge with great credit, showing both forbearance and understanding. The college was obviously torn between a natural, indeed an obligatory, desire to get a reasonable return from the estate and their recognition that Waterperry Horticultural School was a truly educational venture and one that they wished to help. Insecurity, both real and imagined, together with the perennial lack of money on the tenant side led to constant problems and some friction. When Miss Havergal wished to plough up more of the Warren, the parkland in front of the house, in order to plant roses, one of her abiding passions, the then Bursar, Arnold J. Forster refused permission with a pointed reminder of the "Liability of pleasure gardens." More practical requests were met. In 1934 the Bursar was delighted to hear that numbers had increased, and raised no objection to the temporary partition of a bedroom. A new archway into the walled garden was permitted, with the proviso that the wall was to be rebuilt at the end of the tenancy or a door installed. Miss Havergal was toying with the idea of planting the two river fields with fruit and this was approved, though the plan never materialized. In November 1935 the rent was actually deferred. 'I greatly regret to hear of your bad luck,' wrote Mr Forster, 'College will allow you till not later than the end of January for the payment of rent due.' What form this particular bad luck took is not recorded, but no doubt the elements played a part. The financial situation was always precarious. In June 1937 the Bursar pointed out, perhaps in reply to another demand, that, with the then rent of £160 per annum, the College had received a net return of £96 in five years and, with the erection of an additional glasshouse, had in fact incurred a loss of £64 over that period.

But in spite of these irritations the College never really lost faith in the eventual success of the school, and did everything possible to further it. The University with all its Botanical and Agricultural resources was an obvious Mecca for Beatrix Havergal, and she set about trying to establish a link between the practical aspects and the theory of Horticulture, something she strove to do all her life and which seems eminently desirable, yet not always fully recognized even today when paper qualifications are so prized. In August 1938, with every assistance from A. J. Forster, she sent a long memorandum to Professor Osborn who held the Chair of Botany and Agriculture at Oxford, and to the President of Magdalen. It was a plea for Waterperry in particular but also for the future of Horticulture in general, and is worth quoting in full.

> Every effort should be made on the part of those concerned with Horticultural Education to provide students with sound scientific knowledge and ample practical skill to enable them to apply it to actual crop production. This presents difficulties in the organization of the syllabus.
>
> At present there are two qualifications open to students of horticulture, a B.Sc.Hort;, taking three years, and the N.D.H., six years practical gardening including two or three years training at an approved centre. Owing to the value of qualifications, economy in the duration of fees and the need for scientific knowledge, many are encouraged to take the B.Sc., and the syllabus gives little time for practical work. Holders qualify for posts in research, as teachers of gardening and Nature Study in schools, but because they have no practical knowledge the majority are not finding it easy to fill important positions in horticulture until experience is gained in crops.
>
> It is usual after the degree to try to get a practical post which

> helps the work for the N.D.H. This is not easy because the N.D.H. syllabus is less exacting on the scientific side but full and up to date knowledge is needed with practical ability. This is important for the top jobs such as County Advisors and Inspectors, and the Royal Horticultural Society has more entrants year by year; however the standard of practical ability is not sufficiently advanced, the practical part of courses being inadequate to meet the needs. In a subject needing practical wisdom and natural understanding there is a need to fill the gap between the theoretical and practical that is of paramount importance, and more so because of the need for increased food production in time of war.
>
> The Waterperry training has been laid out to meet the requirements of the National Diploma, approved by the Royal Horticultural Society, and the Ministry of Agriculture with the Inspector of Education for Oxfordshire have been highly appreciative. Unless, however, facilities can be given to enable students to combine this course with their study for the B.Sc. Hort. at existing Universities or Colleges, it will be difficult to obtain sufficient students to make it financially possible to continue this institution, notwithstanding the very generous assistance given by Magdalen College in the terms upon which the property is lent to us.
>
> If this view commends itself to the University, I would like to suggest that facilities be given to students in Botany to attend an approved course of practical training at Waterperry with a grant for that purpose from the University, thus enabling them to qualify for a B.Sc. Hort. Apart from the value to any student in Botany it would go a long way towards qualification for both the B.Sc. Hort and the N.D.H., the combination of which is so desirable in all candidates for positions of importance in practical horticulture.

It is useless to speculate on what might have been the effect on Waterperry at this stage if the University had acted on Miss Havergal's proposals, and one wonders if she would really have been willing to surrender a fraction of her personal control. However it was not to be, and 1938 was not the easiest of years in which to contemplate future strategies. Thoughts of war, temporarily lulled by the Munich agreement, were in the Bursar's mind when he wrote in that anxious September, 'I very much hope that this crisis, which at last seems to be showing signs of clearing, will have brought home to the Ministry the national importance of the work you are doing, and thus enable you to achieve the success in its development you deserve. In November he wrote another sympathetic letter giving the University's decision. 'I am extremely sorry to have to tell you that there is no hope of the University being able to give you any help. Your memorandum has been very sympathetically considered by Professor Osborn, but after discussion with his departmental colleagues he has come to the conclusion that neither the Botanical nor the Agricultural Departments could start a B.Sc. Hort. Course.'

Chapter Five

The outbreak of war in 1939 found the Waterperry Horticultural School established and growing in reputation, though still in low water financially. Regarding the last condition perhaps one can discern a hopeful note in a letter from the Magdalen College Bursar. 'In view of the outbreak of war you will probably be badly wanted in connection with food production.' The war certainly created problems for Waterperry as it did for all, but there is no doubt that it also provided a very useful stimulus. But another institution was to present a different type of threat, and few people know how close the school was to extinction in 1940 and 1941.

In 1940 the John Innes Horticultural Institute had approached Magdalen College with a view to stepping in at the end of the Havergal-Sanders lease, and turning Waterperry into the permanent home of the Institute. They would take over the College's tenancy obligations to the Principals in respect of accommodation and tenants' rights, and were prepared to allow Miss Havergal the use of all glasshouses then standing and the land, apart from about thirty-one acres. She could also remain in occupation of most of the house and the grounds at a rent of £150 per annum, and would be paid a fee for selective cultivations on behalf of the John Innes, together with half the profits. But, although she could occupy the house until John Innes entered into full possession the Institute would require some rooms immediately. This unexpected menace came as a fearful shock to the partners. They had faced the real difficulties of the move from compact Pusey to the undeveloped acres of Waterperry, they had, together with their helpers, tightened their belts and lived frugally while working incredibly hard, and they were just beginning to see the emergence of the school they had dreamed of. Now this school's very existence was suddenly threatened by a large well-to-do impersonal institution; the thought that they might have to start again on another property, or even give up altogether must have given them many sleepless nights.

Full records of the correspondence involved were not kept at the Waterperry end, but the new College Bursar, Mark Dunbar Van Oss, displayed great patience and diplomacy as the man in the middle. It seems fitting that the name Van Oss has been remembered in Waterperry Church on every Remembrance Sunday since the war, for Mark's brother, Thomas, was one of the two men of the village not to return. Scraps of correspondence give the flavour of the episode in question. Placating an obviously furious Miss Havergal, Van Oss comments that Magdalen were unable to give way to personal considerations. He reminds her that an Act of Parliament governed University Estates and that 'every lease shall reserve the best rent that can reasonably be obtained.' He pleads with her to employ a solicitor to act for her, to prevent misunderstandings, probably an understatement! He is not above a little dig; having discussed the question of valuation of goodwill he writes, 'it is very difficult to suggest a basis as your accounts have not usually shown a profit.' Obviously the Principals were in a very difficult position, faced with gradual erosion of room space and rights, and with the eventual extinction of their school. 'It would be impossible to work without the house,' Miss Havergal writes to Van Oss, 'we could not pay rent without students, and could not employ staff without glasshouses.' The thought of John Innes employees, male, actually living in the house obviously horrifies both ladies. 'We should find it impossible to house gardeners, viz. ordinary working men — they must be boarded out in the village.' Uncertainty and doubt seems to have bedevilled the affair on both sides. On 7th February Van Oss writes, 'I am very glad you are now protected by a solicitor — would he like to see me and see the file? It is important to decide once and for all about the position with the College, as until this is clear the whole business with the John Innes Institute is hampered by some degree of uncertainty as to what line you are going to take.' The Institute caused Van Oss equal alarm. 'Between ourselves,' he writes to Miss Havergal, 'Mr L . . . . . seems to have only the vaguest instructions from the John Innes Institute, and nobody seems to be clear as to how far his authority goes. Nor is any contract yet definitely signed. In the circumstances I shall be obliged if you will keep me informed as to the nature and progress of his schemes as I do not want anything to be done without being sure that a) it will be supported by the Institute and b) will not be likely to spoil Waterperry.'

Magdalen College at one time anticipated the transfer with a request which brings back memories of those war years. Van Oss wrote to say that Magdalen were turfing their front Quad, having thought it safer to remove flagstones and concrete foundations which might act 'as a bursting course for bombs!' They were lifting turf for the purpose from the College meadow and wished to replace it; could they have turf from 'the triangle' at Waterperry, probably to be cultivated with a view to John Innes taking over? As we know, the University with its colleges came through unscathed without the benefit of Waterperry turf, and the 'triangle' presumably the lawn near the church and under the study window, is green to this day.

The John Innes Institute were so confident of success that in their Annual Report of 1940 the Directors wrote that there had been agreement on the lease of Waterperry House, plus sixty-three acres as the permanent home of the Institute. 'This handsome and well-designed mansion would,' they wrote, 'with its fifty rooms, provide them with 12,000 square feet of floor space, and allow all offices, libraries, lecture rooms, laboratories, stores, etc. to be under one roof.' The park and garden gave the house an admirable setting, of which they would be able to take advantage. The report continues, rather patronizingly, 'Waterperry is at present occupied by the Waterperry Horticultural School which trains girls in practical gardening. It is managed by Miss Havergal and Miss Sanders who will continue to cultivate the land and occupy the house until the Institute can enter into possession.'

Magdalen College, to their eternal credit, clearly felt under a moral obligation to the two Principals as tenants who, although they had had concessions over rent, had greatly improved the grounds and were fully engaged in an educational enterprise. On the other hand Mark Van Oss admitted to Miss Havergal that the proposed letting to the John Innes was of course more advantageous financially, and beyond that there was probably advantage to the cause of science in Oxford. He openly hopes for compromise. 'I hope that, while watchfully guarding your interests you will give very serious considerations to any proposals that may be put forward. I believe you will find it best to state boldly the terms which you want, and leave it to them to say how far they can meet you.' Privately Van Oss was not so sanguine about the possibility of compromise. The Institute took the line that they would be using Miss Havergal's expertise; she, on the other hand, could see herself as little better than a caretaker. Hope of co-operation, wrote Van Oss — who knew his Havergal — to her solicitor, 'must, at the best, be regarded as doubtful.'

Negotiations eventually foundered on the question of legal liabilities to the Horticultural School. E. A. Courthorpe, Trustee of John Innes, writing to Van Oss states quite clearly that the Institute would never agree to any lease saddling the Trustees with such liabilities, while prepared to make quite fair terms. 'We are doing far more than any other prospective tenant of Waterperry House is likely to do, i.e. we are ready to keep Miss Havergal going for a time, and the College knows we are ready to do so. We demand vacant possession and have given the College an assurance of our benevolent intentions, but I refuse to give any legal undertaking to this in the lease.' On the 29th October a most welcome note reached Waterperry from Van Oss, 'I have heard unofficially that the John Innes are very unlikely to pursue the transaction further.' The final capitulation came with the publication of the John Innes Report with a correction slip over all — 'owing to difficulties in reaching agreement negotiations for the lease of Waterperry have broken down.'

The Institute had, rather surprisingly considering the uncertainties of the situation, already begun to move stock to Waterperry, and their men had been duly lodged in the village while they planted 150 fruit stocks and 500 blackberries. Board and lodging for two men for five days in 1941 came to £3-11-6, the men's own wages varying from 10/- a day to 6/3 and 5/5. The spoils of this engagement remained with Miss Havergal who was given the fruit stocks for her own use; the blackberries were eventually lifted again and returned to the Institute at Merton.

This skirmish was of course being carried on against the background of a real war, and the ladies of Waterperry threw themselves wholeheartedly into the task of providing food, while at the same time trying to keep the educational aspect alive and the training programmes as intact as possible. The sedate ladylike atmosphere of the house received a breath of fresh air with the arrival of Land Army personnel, women of varying ages and experience coming for short courses. Several of these who came for a few weeks were to stay for years and play a great part in the building up of the school. Food production was of vital importance, but a certain amount of ornamental gardening was still allowed by the watchful War Agricultural Committee for training purposes. In this new atmosphere Waterperry throve. When the John Innes dust had settled Miss Havergal took in twenty-five acres of the West Field, running in a direct line from the front door, beyond the park. This land was ploughed by the 'War Ag.' — as it was universally known — together with four and a half acres in the river field.

Two carthorses now joined the staff having special requirements, so the five acre pasture running towards Bow Bridge and Waterstock was taken in to provide fodder for them. In 1941 twenty-nine acres were planted with potatoes, the virgin soil producing spectacular results, and two hundred yards of potato clamps for storage. In 1942 they had twelve acres of corn, fewer potatoes but more acres of other vegetables, including an acre of onions. The urgency of the situation led to innovation; amid great excitement a New Fordson tractor arrived. A Cockshutt 10 foot two-furrow plough followed, and they were less dependent on borrowed equipment; Miss Havergal was also wildly excited at the advent of a cabbage planter which involved four sitters-on dropping plants into prepared holes. She also paid a visit to East Malling Research Station and, as a result, launched out into fruit propagation, an acre for East Malling, half an acre for herself and another half acre of raspberry canes. In 1943 200,000 strawberry plants were sent away and hundreds of bundles of canes, all neatly packed in straw. Not to be outdone by these West Field ventures Joan Stokes grew three-quarters of an acre of outdoor tomatoes in the South Field, picking eight tons of fruit.

The remarkable potato crop of 1941 looms large in a magazine article written some years later by Daphne Byrne, entitled 'Land Girl looks back, Oxford 1942'. In it she describes her time at Bellair House, a pun no doubt on the bracing atmosphere, and a thin disguise for Waterperry. The article describes the building. 'Bellair House, built late in the reign of Queen Anne, stands back square in its sombre grey stone amidst beeches and, over the pillared porch, Virginia Creeper climbs to the highest point of the parapet which encircles the roof. Before the house a drive sweeps round to meet fields on one side and the farmhouses and barns on the other. To the north, thirty acres of unprotected land filled with the dense green of potato tops stretches away to the furthest boundaries, and to the south are lawns, greenhouses, a walled-in garden and a stream moving through the water meadows and woods beyond.' The author lists the work done in early September and then returns to those potatoes.

> As the month drew to a close, blight slowly spread across the fields. In turn the War Agricultural Committee, the County Advisers, and the textbooks advised spraying with sulphuric acid, which, in theory, was correct but, in practise, untried. Nevertheless a horse-drawn cart bearing a drum of acid pumped through metal sprayers moved gradually across the river fields, although every few hours the spray pipe deteriorated and had to be replaced. By October the potato lifting had begun.
>
> Furrows were turned up with a double-breasted plough and the

> tops thrown to every sixth furrow, to be carted off and burnt in enormous fires by the river. At first the experience was new, but when the time came to harvest the potato crop in the thirty acre field, where the furrows seemed endless, our enthusiasm blunted. Here we encountered further trouble because the potatoes had been too deeply planted and had to be spun out with a tractor and spinner, with the Army and ourselves following behind picking up the potatoes and putting them into buckets. Added to which frustration the carthorses kicked the gate open and bolted during the night, only to be retrieved by the Home Guard several miles away on the borders of the next county. We were also aware of Canadian soldiers in our midst as one morning, when two of us went to open up the hen house, we found not a bird in sight but, to our enormous pleasure, a bottle of whisky and a five pound note.
>
> By the side of the field soldiers stationed near by assisted us (they got three shillings an hour and we got one shilling and six pence) in building huge clamps of earth to hold two tons of potatoes each for every three square yards, and these were constructed in a trench with soil thrown up to a height of five feet before the final thatching and earthing up of the roof, so that walls everywhere were a foot thick in protection from frost. Needless to say the moles had a field day, amusing themselves by burrowing through the clamps. As the autumn swiftly slipped into winter, and the flames died from the remaining leaves as they fell, the north wind tore over the fields, and potato picking presented a bleak prospect. However we achieved remarkable success, thanks to the aid of the Army and the villagers.

Her experiences on these bleak but productive areas do not seemed to have damped Daphne Byrne's ardour to any great extent as she writes apropos of life in the house, 'we were immensely happy, hard-working, and supremely uncomfortable.' It is not clear why whisky in lieu of the rightful inhabitants of the hen house inevitably meant Canadian marauders, all armies having 'lived off the land' for centuries, but perhaps the brand on the bottle was a clue. No doubt its finders considered it legitimate spoils of war. The Army helpers referred to were usually billeted in Waterstock, and Miss Havergal paid one shilling per head, presumably per day, for their services. At one time soldiers were actually billeted in the loft over the marketing shed; this move must have enlivened Waterperry considerably, while causing the Principals all kinds of anxieties.

For the regular workers, students and Land Army alike, wartime at Waterperry was both rewarding and exhausting; it was also great fun. The carpet in the ballroom-cum-common-room was often rolled back — with Miss S.'s willing co-operation — for dances, other Waterperry inhabitants and folk from surrounding villages being invited. Sometimes they had fancy dress parties, or arranged socials to raise money for some special war effort such as Buy A Spitfire. Other villages were doing the same and the house dwellers were invited back. Entertainments were, by necessity, home based and those with dramatic talent took up play-acting; these efforts were often produced by Frances Collingwood-Selby, Miss H.'s elder sister. She had considerable skill as befitted a drama teacher, but also an infuriating Gielgudian habit of changing her mind as often as the weather in her search for perfection.

Outside in the early war years the strict rotation work in departments, later to be the linchpin of the training, could not be implemented. The first West Field team as such consisted of Ena Mitchell and Liz Stewart, students, and May King who came for a month and stayed for two years, aided by a helpful good-tempered workman known as Smithy, who acted as foreman and mentor. They produced peas, parsnips, carrots and leeks, and thought nothing of rolling a one-acre onion bed with a large garden roller, two pulling in tandem. When there was a long cold snap in the winter of 1941 they set about digging out an elm tree which stood in the way of cultivation at the end of the West Field, trenching round it and axing roots as they became visible until the tree was loosed sufficiently to be pulled out with a tractor. Not long afterwards the Royal Engineers came to deal with a group of elms, laid charges, and blew them out in one effortless action. That was all too easy and dull and, as Liz Stewart philosophically recorded, they had both enjoyed the work and kept themselves warm. The weather was responsible for another course of action — or inaction — the only strike that Waterperry has ever known. The West Field team found themselves picking frozen sprouts day after day while other students found shelter and warmth in the glasshouses. After several days they flatly refused to do more and after that all took their turn at what can be the most painful of marketing tasks. Ask any former Waterperry student for her most uncomfortable memories and sprout picking in a frost will be at the top of her list.

Waterperry could almost have been described as a Home Farm in the early years of the war. Pigs were fattened in the sties, and in October of 1940 four pampered porkers were dispatched to Brazil and Co., doing their best to improve the wartime 'banger' as a result of a diet of well-cooked potatoes and swill. They brought in over thirty pounds, weighing 28 score 13 lbs at twenty-one shillings to cart them. Waterperry village had its Pig Club with Peggy Chaplin's brother-in-law, Ted Fonge, as Secretary, and with Joan Stokes on the Committee, which ensured that all pig owners got their full rations of Topping and Ground Nuts meal. Hereford and Devon steers were wintered in the yards, and there were hens to feed and eggs, hopefully, to collect; woe betide any student who tried to wriggle out of her poultry duties at weekends in order to indulge in any social activity. The carthorses, Boxer and Dinah, were treasured members of the family. Dinah, the little dip-backed mare, was the more co-operative, and was a dab hand — or foot — at horse-hoeing brassicas, walking patiently and neatly between the rows of plants. Legend has it that she pined for days when her companion, Boxer, had a dangerous attack of colic.

The two horses were needed too for haymaking and harvest. The Horticultural School had few agricultural implements, and Mr Fonge senior — there have been Fonges at Waterperry since 1797 — used to lend his binder and carts, and give advice. Students and Land Army girls did the work, and there are many yellowing photographs still extant of farm carts full of healthy young women, wearing the white shirts and green dungarees that had replaced the summer breeches. These were the days of 'double summer-time', imposed with the farming communities in mind, and often the last loads would come home with the moon just rising, and a very short night in prospect.

In 1942 there were the beginnings of an important development in production when Miss Havergal, whose first love was always fruit, proposed to plant a six-acre orchard in the West Field. This of course required permission from the landlords; it was inevitably a long-term project, and the lease from the College ran out in 1948. From the correspondence available over something as tranquil as an orchard we see glimpses of the ever-present anxieties, financial above all, and of the indecisions. In January 1943 Miss Havergal wrote to Van Oss, 'I am very glad that you agree to our planting the six-acre orchard in the West Field, and I much appreciate your proposal that the trees should be paid for by, and be the property of, the College. Under this arrangement can I assume that the College would be prepared to pay the recognized valuation, i.e. a small sum per tree for every year of our tenancy?' Van Oss replied rather coolly that he was not aware of any recognized valuation of this kind, and Miss Havergal, in reply, must have made some unguarded remarks about her insecurity of tenure and suspicion of the College's intentions.

Van Oss, leaping to the defence of his Trustees, replies that best results will not be obtained without real confidence between herself and the College. Personally he has a high opinion of Miss Havergal's ability, and wants expansion at Waterperry to take full advantage of its exceptional soil (her own discovery), but the College was right to take an interest in the development. He, Van Oss, would recommend the College to give greater security by grant of a longer lease, if they could be satisfied that the Havergal plans were financially sound. Miss Havergal in reply stresses that the new orchard would not repay the labour involved for seven or eight years, and would then be extremely valuable. She has only one desire, to build up Waterperry into a really successful concern, but she wants to feel that it is worth planning and planting up for the future. She is confident that there is a future, provided it is concerned with work of vital importance. Propagation of leading strains of fruit, in connection with the Ministry of Agriculture and East Malling Research Station, would be a sound proposition.

By the time these first apple trees were planted the two Principals were their own mistresses of the land, and Magdalen College had parted with the estate, probably with some relief. But, as their first landlord, the College had played an important part in the early development of the Horticultural School.

Chapter Six

Problems caused by the war did not remain outside on the land. They spilled over into the house, and doubtless rationing made life even more difficult for Avice Sanders, already coping with the tightest of budgets. From that August day, when the little band of pioneers stood in the big hall she was Commander-in-Chief of the house, as Beatrix Havergal was leader out of doors. It cannot be stressed too often that theirs was an equal partnership, yet the more flamboyant Beatrix leaned heavily on Avice who, for all her reticence, was a woman of great character and of rare worth.

There are many photographs of Beatrix Havergal in all phases of her life, in public and private occasions, and a fine posthumous portrait by Charles Hardaker, now in Christopher Havergal's possession. She looms large in the memories of her students, so memorable in breeches, smock and blazer with her cropped white hair, lively eyes behind the round glasses, huge feet in the well polished shoes from Duckers, and a big voice of command, voluble, enthusiastic, and great fun. There are relatively few photographs of Avice Sanders, and even fewer where she faces the camera squarely and smilingly; usually the eyes are dropped or the face averted. She was pleasant in appearance with a strong nose, the reddish hair inherited from her mother's family, and the clear skin that often goes with that colouring, while her eyes could be steely behind her glasses. She was a woman of few words and one who was hard to know, and few students managed to penetrate her reserve. Some found her actually frightening; one unfortunate newcomer mistook her at their first meeting for Miss Havergal's treasured secretary, Hilda Johns, and felt that Avice Sanders never really forgave her, there being some competition between the two women for Beatrix's time and affections. Avice was perhaps a little like an oyster; it took time and careful handling to get to the pearl. Those who lived for many years in the house came to love her as a firm friend, with a twinkle in the eye and a dry sense of humour. She was artistic and had exhibited paintings as a young woman; in direct contrast to her partner she loved clothes and dressed well. Under the sharp exterior she was a woman of great kindness which expressed itself in countless little acts for which she hated to be thanked. Betty Thin, the early 'stalwart', who found the Sanders regime far too rigid, elected to live in a caravan in the old orchard, but had a real fear of thunderstorms. If a storm broke Avice Sanders would always sally forth to keep Betty company, or would check that she was safely in the house. Staff who stayed over Easter would find little gifts by their plates on Easter morning, a posy of flowers or a nest of chocolate eggs. She despised malingerers, showing superb disregard for her own ailments, but could be kindness itself in cases of real illness.

It seems right to put Avice Sanders in the forefront at this stage when she first began her reign in the house. In the latter years of the school honours came thick and fast, but only for Beatrix Havergal; few outsiders knew her partner and this was as Avice wanted it. But there seems little doubt that this self-effacing woman was the stabilizing force, the 'Power House' as one former student described her, and the quiet background that Beatrix Havergal needed. She, of the pair, was the decisive one. She was not present at staff or student interviews, and would slip out of other gatherings with the excuse of 'something on the stove' but she provided the still centre of this very concentrated and unique little world.

Naturally self-disciplined, almost to fanaticism, Avice Sanders expected this in others, and was fully prepared to impose it if necessary. One weakness in both Principals was an inability to provide more than a boarding-school atmosphere: Avice had been a pupil at Downe House with her sisters before returning there as domestic staff, and one feels that they never visualized Waterperry as anything other than an extension of school. Even their staff had to conform, and were expected to report on return from an evening outing. They remained pre-war in attitude to their students, and this undoubtedly caused friction as a more emancipated generation arrived. The shyer girls felt protected and at home, the more independent spirits would have preferred more freedom, come what may.

Certainly domestic order was needed in this lively all-female establishment, and Avice Sanders provided it with an almost obsessive fondness for routine and a terrifying eye for detail. The roomy old-fashioned kitchen was run on martial lines; students on the serving rota approached through one door and went thankfully out of the other laden with dishes. A tea-towel tucked negligently under the arm ready for washing up would be instantly whipped away with a brusque "insanitary". Food for the dining-room arrived on a none too young trolley, and had to be wheeled along beflagged and uneven corridors. 'Pull, not push' is a dictum that echoed down those corridors year after year as earnest anxious first years shot the kippers on to the flagstones. Rather endearing glimpses of 'Miss S.' linger in students' memories, a 'rigid back stirring the buttered eggs' as seen by Brenda Jones. Several probably still carry trays by the 'Sanders' method, with one hand slid to the centre to steady the load. To be fair to Miss S. thrift and care lay behind all her strictures, and she would have been horrified to know that her successors in the house broke almost the entire set of blue and white china that she had kept intact for over thirty years in a short space of time. All breakages had, of course, to be reported, and certain brave spirits or those who 'got on' with Avice Sanders were detailed by more timid fellows to brave the lion. This brusqueness of manner spilled over into physical action; she would, for example, serve pudding from the side-board at top speed seldom lifting her eyes from the dish, and expecting the plate to be ready to receive the portion. On one occasion a wicked student quietly withdrew with the last plate of prunes without warning, with the hoped-for messy result. In the same way she would whirlwind round the bedrooms with clean linen, hurling it with precision and never a backward glance on to the beds. Hilary Fletcher remembers being winded by a well-directed pair of sheets when lying on her bed feeling unwell, quite unnoticed by the sender. Miss S. also had a fixation over furniture and had a built-in mental inventory of the contents — and the position of the contents — of all the bedrooms. Woe betide the student who decided that she preferred her bed on the other side of the room.

All this rigidity and passion for order would seem to make Avice Sanders a somewhat unattractive figure, and those who were themselves too shy or too brash to understand her probably found her so. "Dear Miss S., how we took her for granted," and "her bark much worse than her bite," were more thoughtful comments from students looking back. Perhaps an anecdote from her last days, related to the writer by her sister Joan, will serve to illustrate the affection in which Avice was held by her closest colleagues, and shed some light on her character. When her health began to fail and she had a slight stroke Avice was away from Waterperry for some time convalescing with her sister. During these weeks a new housekeeper had perforce to be called in, and life in the house went on as usual. Driving Avice back to Waterperry Joan Sanders knew that her sister was nervous and unhappy about her possible reception; would she even be wanted, and would there still be a place for her? The car drew quietly up to the pillared entrance, and Avice walked into the portico. At once the big front door was flung open and a tiny figure hurled herself out, throwing her arms round Avice and crying, "Welcome home," Joan Stokes had watched and waited to make sure that her misgivings were unnecessary, and that she had been missed from her place in the family. The plaque now in Waterperry Church above the pew near the door where she so often slipped in unnoticed, reads 'Remember Avice Sanders — much loved' and for many that rings true.

The house itself, old and rambling, was not the easiest of buildings to command, but it had the graciousness and welcoming atmosphere of a family home. Shy girls away from home for the first time and perplexed by the confusion of corridors and staircases soon lost any feelings of strangeness. There were no ghosts to lay — though a certain chair was supposed to rock gently at night without a visible occupant; any other scuttlings could be traced to chewed-up scraps in waste-paper baskets and to small holes in the skirting boards. The house's history, such as is known, is predominantly domestic, but succeeding owners ran to a very consistent pattern; they were religious, firmly royalist, and prone to suffer from financial crises.

The present house was built by Sir John Curson towards the end of Queen Anne's reign, probably on the site of a medieval building the only trace of which is the fourteenth century arched doorway of stone. The wing jutting out on the east and forming one side of the little churchyard is older, and was listed in 1665 as having nine hearths. The Cursons, related to the more illustrious Curzons of Kedleston, were an old Derbyshire family who held the manor for two hundred years, having set out to acquire it almost by stealth. The first Curson to settle in Waterperry was Walter who, although he never owned the property and who died four years after he was granted the lease in 1523, is depicted twice in the church and who, even more importantly for the church, left a sound roof over his memorials. Walter and his eight sons kneel in the sixteenth century window high in the lord's aisle, facing his wife Isabel and their six or perhaps seven daughters. Walter and Isabel are also the subjects of the intriguing palimpsest — or twice-used — brass at the entrance to the chancel. In the early sixteenth century Walter was busy acquiring land in Oxfordshire and Buckinghamshire, leasing two hundred acres from the Foster family descended by marriage from the Beaufeus, much earlier owners of Waterperry, and no doubt biding his time for the place itself. But it was not until 1562 that Walter's grandson, Vincent, was able to buy Waterperry after the then owner, George Tyrell, had according to County records 'impaired the family estate very much and squandered away several manors.'

Francis succeeded Vincent, acquired a knighthood and a splendid mural tablet in the church sanctuary, and it was Vincent's grandson, John, who fought for his king during the Civil War and spent some time in the Tower for his pains. He had been knighted by Charles I in Whitehall in 1641 and was one of the gentlemen who met at the Star Hotel in Oxford's Cornmarket to plan for the city's defence. Not long after he was captured by the Roundheads while trying to seize the magazine at Wallingford, and Hampden sent him to the Tower. A petition for his release was eventually submitted on grounds of his age and because the estate 'was suffering much from his absence.' His second son, William, also fought for the king, and was twice 'wanted' for horse stealing, presumably for the Royalist cavalry. Only one son survived Sir John, namely Thomas who was created Baronet after the Restoration and became Sheriff of Oxfordshire. It was Thomas's son, another John, who rebuilt Waterperry House, beginning in 1713.

Sir John's house with its three storeys, its balustraded parapet, the seven bays on the west front and the north, must have impressed the neighbours and local worthies. Sadly only one more direct generation succeeded. John's heir, Francis, died childless and the last of the Curson male line was his brother, Peter, a Jesuit priest. Perhaps the realization that the family had failed to found a dynasty was responsible for the permanent record on the main staircase. Portraits of various Cursons, painted in the schools of Sir Peter Lely and Sir Godfrey Kneller, have looked down disapprovingly on domestics or horticultural students who dared to risk using this staircase instead of clattering down the narrow uncarpeted back flights. The Cursons were not a handsome family, if the likenesses were true; the latest are thought to have been painted about 1727, and are probably those of Sir Francis and his two wives. They have survived the latest changes in the house's fortunes, and have emerged cleaner and brighter from the ordeal, if with no more animation. A descendant, a Roper-Curson, was interested in buying them when the estate changed hands in 1971, but, quite rightly, they remain in their own house.

The Cursons remained loyal to their King in time of rebellion; most of them remained loyal to the Catholic faith after the Reformation. Waterperry was a staunch centre of Roman Catholicism as was Stonor, the home of the Camoys family near Henley-on-Thames. The first Curson recusant recorded as having been fined was a Walter Curson in

London in 1577. Francis Curson's wife, Ann, formerly Southcote, with whom he kneels in their Jacobean tablet in the church, was fined four times, while two of their daughters became nuns. Ann was influenced by the great preacher John Gerard, entertained him frequently and fell entirely under his spell; it seems that her husband was either more worldly or more circumspect. Undoubtedly there were Jesuits at Waterperry in the seventeenth century since, when England became a Jesuit province, it was one of six centres of mission organized in Oxfordshire. When Sir John Curson rebuilt the house in 1713 several coffins were discovered under the foundations, one of these covered in black velvet and containing a silver crucifix and candlestick. Sir John himself was converted back to Rome — the family had lapsed earlier, perhaps for expediency — by his first wife, and his second wife was also a Catholic; he figures in Hearnes' *Remarks and Collections* as 'a man that was a Catholic but of great goodness.' Throughout the eighteenth century the house maintained its private chapel, situated on the south-east corner which forms an apse, and priests from several Catholic orders lived in the house. These historical facts have led to the romantic if vague belief that the house boasts a secret tunnel as escape route for heroic fugitives, but none has ever been found.

With the death of Peter Curson, the Jesuit, the estate passed to a niece who took the name of Curson but died unmarried, two other heirs and finally to Francis Henry Roper, who took the name of Roper-Curson, and later became the 14th Baron Teynham. Unfortunately he was a confirmed gambler and his losses eventually obliged him to part with the estate. In 1815 Waterperry was sold to a Mr Joseph Henley, a London merchant. The first Henley to advance in the world had sailed from County Cork as a cabin boy, arrived in London and flourished as a Thames waterman. His son went further by water, and discovered something about Mediterranean tides that was of benefit to a grateful Government. The next Henley went into the coal trade and became a ship owner, trading with the East Indies. The first Joseph Henley at Waterperry altered Sir John's windows and added the central portico of three bays to the west front, stamping his crest, suitably an anchor, on the cast iron rainwater heads to announce his arrival. He also dismantled the family chapel, the action perhaps of a firm Protestant or of a hard-headed business man, and embellished the window of the main staircase with the chapel glass. His son, Joseph Warner Henley, was a prominent figure both locally and nationally, a member of Parliament for more than thirty years, and twice President of the Board of Trade. Two more Joseph Henleys succeeded and it was Captain Joseph Henley, RN who sold the estate to Magdalen College in 1925, by which time Mrs O'Connor was occupying the house.

From the moment Avice Sanders followed Mrs O'Connor and was deposited, with her partner and companions, in the big hall she must have realized the enormity of her task, certainly a burden that she could never lay down. From the start the big room at the head of the main staircase was to be the Principals' bedroom, probably the only place where they could confer in private. It was also rumoured that Beatrix Havergal could check the impeccably straight lines of the herbaceous frames as she knotted her tie at the window each morning. Close by was the ballroom where Lily O'Connor had snuggled down in her four-poster, and which the students had for their common-room. This room had made a considerable impression on the Land Army worker, Daphne Byrne. In her article she wrote, 'Occasionally we would have lectures in our beautiful common-room, with a vast expanse of sherry-coloured carpet below and exquisite crystal chandeliers above, and usually there was a log fire burning in a marble fireplace whose mantelpiece was supported by long suffering Grecian maidens. Sometimes from sheer boredom we "made them up" and forgot about them until during a lecture we became aware that their momentary glamour had been removed.' Here the students could relax, play table-tennis, gossip and grumble like all other students. The organ was removed, but replaced by an excellent grand piano, available to any who dared to use it. The ballroom is a beautiful room with a central bay window, looking out over the parkland and on to the expanses of the West Field, but the fireplaces at either end did little to soften the icy blasts between them in winter; conditions upstairs were certainly spartan, high ceilings in the bedrooms adding to the discomforts. Students over the years grumbled and shivered, and the more pampered post-war generations expected more comfort; the 1958 group rebelled to such effect that electric heaters were installed in the bedrooms. The electricity bills soared so high that the heaters were switched off long before the end of winter. Hot water was by no means a certainty and the bathrooms boarded and bare, while laundry facilities were, for a long time, practically non-existent. The Principals came from the generation and class who sent out their washing; the advent of man-made fibres, stream-lined underclothing and financial expediency made that system impossible, but it was some years before even an iron was installed and then only under protest.

Next to the ballroom was the library, another spacious room lacking in comfort; Daphne Byrne described it as a haunt for dead and dying flies. Here students had lectures in the days before the lecture block was built. At one end a large cupboard housed a fascinating collection of light reading, the novels and classic stories beloved by all girls' boarding-schools between the wars. Here Jeffrey Farnol heroes rubbed shoulders with Ethel M. Dell heroines, the Musketeers and Brigadier Gerard fought their way across Europe, and Florence Barclay's erring nuns suffered with Sorrell and Son. Small beer indeed if compared with such as .007, but perhaps less lethal in their side effects, and the collection as a whole a piece of social history. The horticultural library, such as it was, was ill-equipped, and never worthy of the training; although each girl was charged ten shillings a term for library fees few new books were bought, and one fears that the fees all too frequently found their way into general funds. Students tried banding together to buy new books as leaving presents; these often got as far as Miss Havergal's study and stayed there, and neither staff nor students seemed to find the courage to demand that the system be improved.

Downstairs the most important room was the big dining-room, its long windows looking out on to the lawn and South Field. Students are usually hungry, horticultural ones doubly so, especially after an hour's work outside before breakfast. One long refectory type table took the centre, Miss H. presiding at the head, Miss S. at the opposite end closest to the kitchen. The Principals were invariably referred to by their initials by staff and students alike, though no would have dreamed of using such an address to them personally. Two or three small tables were under the window and, while senior staff had more or less permanent places on the top table junior staff and students were required to rotate, taking their turns beside each Principal. The prospect of a meal by the monosyllabic Miss S. was daunting, and attempts were made to evade the ordeal only to be thwarted by the lady herself. Before the war everyone had her napkin in its individual ring, the patterns of which all had to be memorized and laid strictly according to rule by those detailed to lay up tables. Miss S. would cast her eye over the table just before the meal and, without a word or even change of expression would alter any napkin that had strayed out of place. During the war and until rationing had finished napkins were dispensed with for economy; the layers-up had instead to remember each individual's butter saucer and marmalade pot, to be laid by the correct place and cleared from the table between meals.

Food is always a most important item in community life, and opinions are divided as to the quality of Miss S.'s catering. The menus, influenced no doubt by boarding-school experience, seldom varied from week to week. However tastes change and fashions too, even in eating habits; the early students thought they were fed splendidly, the later ones considered the food to be dreadful. There were the comic and remembered disasters, such as the morning when the porridge mysteriously became mixed with left-over onion soup. Miss S.'s fish pie and kedgeree were greeted with suspicion, and Henry Guy always maintained that it was a miracle that anyone survived the mince; before he became Shop Manager he was frequently carrying drinking water into the kitchen when that dish was being prepared. On the other hand many remember splendid salads, real coffee on Sunday mornings, and delicious Saturday suppers. One genuine complaint was that the best produce invariably went to the shop and the house made do with rejected vegetables and bruised fruit. The conclusion seems to be that Miss S. was a first-class cook constrained within a third-class budget.

She certainly spent much of her time in her kitchen coping splendidly, if a little fiercely, with her houseful of young women of varying backgrounds and temperaments, and all in a large cold building. She must have longed sometimes for a little more comfort, perhaps even a mechanical aid or two. But by mutual consent and quite ungrudged by Miss S. any profit was immediately ploughed back into the horticultural side; the sale of cattle one year produced a new glasshouse, a bumper crop managed to buy a new tractor. Miss S.'s reward was an occasional splash of distemper to brighten up her kitchen walls. Her housekeeping was impeccable, even down to the cellars. When the County Fire Service did a survey of the house in 1952 with the object of checking for possible fire dangers and suggesting an escape system, the report noted that the basement was 'exceedingly clean, and without the usual accumulation of various combustible materials,' and the housekeeping throughout the premises was considered to be exceptionally good. Needless to say the Fire Service Report was never acted upon. There was no money for fire escapes and, fortunately, no Safety Officer in those days to press the point, though it might have been prudent to have had an occasional Fire Drill. Miss S.'s 'exceedingly clean cellars' were the subject of correspondence with Magdalen College in 1941. The College was considering the removal of its pictures from Hall and elsewhere to a place of greater safety, and the Waterperry cellars were offered as a possible refuge, together with careful measurements of the entrance. Perhaps this was not sufficient as there is no record of any unusual refugees being housed.

One member of Avice Sanders's staff who must have appreciated her dedication and her love of routine was the 'Clock Man', Mr Grain. He owned a small family shop in Headington, selling and mending clocks, watches, and small items of jewellery. Every Wednesday, his early closing day, he caught the afternoon bus to the Waterstock turn on the Thame Road, and walked up past the Mill, over Bow Bridge, and past South Lodge to the house. Here he moved quietly through the rooms winding up the eight-day clocks, finishing with the one in the kitchen where he accepted a cup of tea from Miss S. Finally he made his way back down the Waterstock Road to catch his return bus. The beginnings of this contract are lost, suitably, in the passage of time; indeed the gentleman became so invisible that no one is quite certain whether he continued to come until the last Wednesday of all. But week after week, year after year, he made his faithful journey whatever the weather unless deep snow prevented his bus from running. One hopes he had a sense of humour. Only Miss S. would know, but if so these two reticent routine lovers must have had a few quiet chuckles over their countless cups of tea before returning to the noise and bustle of their separate worlds.

Chapter Seven

One direct result of the war was that well-known institution, the Waterperry shop in Oxford's covered market. The 1937 School Prospectus had included a Marketing Section as an integral part of the training. It reads: 'As the Gardens supply Fruit and Vegetables to many customers in Oxford, including Colleges, students have excellent opportunities of learning first-class marketing. All kinds of cut flowers and plants have to be grown during the year to meet the increasing demand of our stall in Swindon Market.'

The Swindon stall every Friday provided a valuable outlet for surplus produce, increasing with the years, and was a perfect training ground in the skill of presenting this produce in the most attractive way. When petrol rationing came into force at the outbreak of war the journey was no longer possible, and the school needed a closer outlet. The covered market in Oxford was the obvious place and Miss Havergal rented a stall, not in the fine central position so well known to Oxford residents later, but down one of the side alleys, rather cramped and dark. At first students took it in turns to man the venture. Then in February, 1942 a Land Army trainee, Irene Willis, came to Waterperry for her four weeks' training and was an instant success on the marketing side. Together with Mavis Goodhew who had come through the auspices of the Women's Farm and Garden Guild she soon took charge of the marketing and saw it through to the end of the war.

By sheer chance the writer arranged to meet Irene Willis, now Irene Collins, at Waterperry on 6th June, 1984, the day Britain and Europe were celebrating the fortieth anniversary of the D-Day landings, and talked with her while sitting in the South Field on a gloriously sunny day. Here Irene had been marketing on that memorable day in 1944, watching the distinctively marked gliders going over Waterperry on their way to France and thinking, privately, that hers had been a marvellous way to spend a war. Quite apart from the satisfaction of being fully engaged in a vital part of the war effort the emergence of the Waterperry shop was a very real cause for pride. Wartime conditions turned produce selling from an educational exercise to a real commercial venture.

For once Waterperry started with a few advantages. As an educational establishment they had the labour necessary for good presentation; while, for instance, other growers merely dug their root vegetables, Waterperry dug, washed and bunched. Their produce was always fresh and attractive, and could boast of a wider range. Unfamiliar and exotic vegetables such as endive, salsify, celeriac and scorzonera, all grown as part of the comprehensive training, appeared on the shelves and were snapped up by more culinary-conscious foreigners who crowded Oxford in wartime. Luxuries like asparagus, tomatoes and strawberries in their seasons lured customers from their habitual stalls.

Running a shop of any kind, whether in war or peace, is hard work; a produce stall must rank among the most difficult and demanding given the fragility of the wares, and the short time desirable between harvesting and the customers' kitchens. Irene, Mavis and their helpers worked hard long hours trying to ensure that Oxford kitchens had the best. Produce of course varied with each month, but the general routine remained constant. Mondays, not a stall day, was almost entirely given over to potato sorting in the big barn, dividing them into the three categories, ware, pig and chip. Ware were the tubers suitable for the average customer, pig were small or damaged and stayed at base to be sold to local pigkeepers, chips of course were the very large tubers and much in demand. All had to be bagged, weighed and recorded. On one trip to Oxford on a Tuesday after a good 'sort' and using, for some reason, a Wheatley builder's lorry the vehicle disintegrated just after crossing Magdalen Bridge and scattered precious potatoes over the famous High. Nothing daunted, one of the team ran to the market for the shop trolley and they pushed their sacks to their destination, no doubt surprising the inhabitants of Queens College and All Souls.

Irene and Mavis were helped with their marketing by the West Field teams, and they soon learnt by experience how many crates of lettuce or cabbage to cut, how many bunches of carrots, baby beet or radish to be pulled and tied. Anyone who has been involved in the marketing of vegetables, or bunching flowers or tying up bundles of raspberry canes will know how important it is to be able to count; in fact former Waterperry girls now pulling their vegetables as housewives in their own gardens will find themselves counting as they do so. Good organization helped to speed things along. If asked for example to pull four dozen bunches of baby beetroot — the dozen still reigned supreme at that time

— the marketer would first cut forty-eight 'strings' short lengths to be used for tying the bunches, not too long as that would be wasteful of string, and not so short as to be fiddly and time-consuming. The 'strings' were then tucked into the belt and the marketer stood astride the row of beet, pulled the six largest within reach, tied them neatly and always with two turns round the necks, and dropped the bunch at the side of the row. This process was repeated at speed down the row, pulling, tying, dropping, until all the strings had been used. The bunches were then picked up, counted and packed neatly into the wooden bushel boxes, all of which were marked with the school's name; the produce was finally hauled up through the gardens on flat trolleys to be washed in the marketing shed sink. This operation involving the handling of 288 beet would be just one small item on the list, and the marketer might then handle the same number of bunches of carrots but with twelve to a string, continuing with radish. The latter were secured with rubber bands previously slipped on one finger to detriment of the circulation, and required deft fingers and the ability to count up to twenty. Fingers and wits were fully employed at speed throughout the long day until the last box or crate was ready in the marketing shed to be loaded up for the following 'shop day'

A shop day meant a six-o-clock start, and Irene and Mavis usually found Joan Stokes already in the shed lifting bunches of flowers out of their baths of water and packing them into boxes, or perhaps laying the beautiful curly chrysanthemum blooms into their long cardboard coffins, a roll of padding under their necks so that the precious petals made no contact with the box. Her colourful pot plants would be transported in trays, each tray padded with newspaper to accommodate the varying size of the pot. In the winter pot plants were always a worry, coming as they did from the comfort of their heated houses. On one especially icy day the Waterperry van broke down outside George's Café at Wheatley, often a haven for hungry students at weekends. Part of the load that day was a large consignment of cineraria which had been cleared from one of the houses. The only alternative transport was an open lorry which, in the sub-zero temperature, quickly became a hearse.

After arrival at the market and unloading the precious produce, all of which had to be pushed to the stall from the lorry park and which frequently spilled out into the alley itself for lack of space, Irene and Mavis would go for breakfast at Hunt's Café, a real breakfast even in wartime and one that was very welcome after such an early start. The egg ration in those days was one a week per person, and Miss Sanders's routine menus ensured that the egg breakfast fell always on a shop day. Fortunately a hen with a well-developed sense of fair play elected to lay daily in the potato barn, and the splendid proprietor of Hunts was only too happy to cook the eggs when the two girls arrived with their spoils. By 8.30 there was usually a queue outside the stall, and the morning passed in a hectic round of selling. The afternoons were quieter, and one of them could take surplus lettuce or other vegetables round to hotels or restaurants always on the look out for quality. Orders were taken on Thursdays for Friday, and these were faithfully delivered even with petrol shortages. Like all shopkeepers who take an interest in their customers Irene and Mavis had their favourites, and items in short supply were often tucked under the counter to wait for the right person. Barter with other traders was quite in order and of mutual benefit. The enterprising pair found that a pound or two of strawberries prompted offers of surplus cake from the Cadena in Cornmarket, a great boon to the hungry as Miss Sanders was no cake maker and resorted to buying rather dreary slab. In Timothy Whites in nearby Queen Street delicacies did much to improve the situation regarding toilet rolls for the house, a perennial problem in the war. Many of the regular customers took an interest in the welfare of the hard-working girls behind the stall. One charming South African lady, caught in this country by the hostilities, was so impressed that on more than one occasion she gave them the run of her Oxford flat, leaving them a supper of delicacies from South African food parcels, and a theatre ticket under the plate. She even hired a taxi to take her out to Waterperry to see for herself the conditions under which they were living, and pronounced herself satisfied.

The two seldom had time for such evenings out. Apart from selling at the stall records had to be kept of sales, and a careful note made of orders. The proceeds from the day went into the old tin money-box — shades of Pusey — and was carried home triumphantly at the end of the day to be counted by Miss Havergal, or by Hilda Johns, her secretary. It was years before Miss Havergal could be persuaded to abandon the money-box ritual, even when changing mores and a considerable rise in takings called for the security of the Bank. Hilda Johns, that efficient and meticulous lady, was often offended by the condition of the shop order books, invariably marked with grubby fingers and with grains of soil between the pages. Nor did she always approve of the extent to which Irene and Mavis trusted their customers and allowed them goods on 'tick', a good old-fashioned custom which was very seldom abused.

Reloading the van with empties, closing the stall and returning to

Waterperry was not the end of the day in the summer months. There was no such thing as 'overtime' and even Miss Sanders relaxed her rule that everyone changed out of working clothes for supper for the shop staff so that they could go out again and do what Irene described as the luxury jobs. Soft fruit was often picked in the cool of the evening when they would be joined by deft-fingered staff such as Joan Stokes and Jo Cockin; all had to be weighed in their punnets, in the case of strawberries lined at the corners with leaves for coolness and effect. Sweet peas and other flowers were cut, bunched, and left to stand overnight in water, the asparagus bed in season was plundered and bunches tied. From that it was a short time before another morning and more marketing to satisfy the appreciative Oxford public. Fridays at the stall found them being encouraged by the two Principals who looked in on their way to their own activities, Miss Sanders to do her weekly shop for the house and Miss Havergal on her way to her weekly meeting of the War Agricultural Committee for the county.

Irene and Mavis certainly laid the foundations for success in the Oxford market, but the original space in the side alley, tucked in by the Women's Institute Stall, could never be expanded. In about 1949 a prime site became vacant and was quickly snapped up by Miss Havergal, and the well-known Waterperry Shop came into being. Not only was it in a light and central position close to the pillar-box for point of reference but it was also on a corner, and so could boast two frontages with a slanted entrance between them. There seems to be no record of the grand opening, who was the first customer, or whether Miss Havergal, bursting with pride and pleasure, welcomed them over the doorstep. It must have been quite an occasion but the memory, like so many other early ones, has been lost. But at last there was light and space enough to show the colourful produce to advantage, both inside and on the shelves in front.

Many Waterperry staff took turns in the Oxford shop over the years but one team was outstanding, that of Honor Shorten, Nora White and Henry Guy, an association that lasted for about sixteen years. Nora White, tall and thin with fierce eyes behind her glasses, a disconcerting stare and a marked Berkshire accent, was perhaps the 'problem child' of the party at times. One of the Whites of Appleton, well-known bell-founders and ringers for generations, she had two pillars in her life, Waterperry and her own garden, and it is difficult to imagine her in any other context. Perhaps she never quite grew up; her handwriting, for example, never progressed beyond printed capitals as her thousands of marketing lists could testify. Undoubtedly she could be difficult to work with, and even alarming to those who did not know her ways; customers of a nervous disposition could be intimidated to the point of desertion, unable to face Nora's brusque condemnation if they had not managed to finish their own digging before Christmas. She was knowledgeable about herbs, and for many years supplied them for Waterperry from her own Appleton garden; on her arrival with a new batch of plants she would proceed to clear her colleagues' careful arrangements of produce left and right so that her own produce could have the central spot. Although she had taken a short course with Constance Spry Nora was an instinctive and intuitive gardener rather than a tutored one, and no doubt her occasional prickliness was a measure of insecurity. But her loyalty to Waterperry and her affection for it could not be faulted, and the association was of immense mutual benefit. After the closure of the Horticultural School and the retirement of Henry Guy Nora lost her landmarks and drifted into depression leading to her tragic death in 1981, much missed by all who admired her industry and devotion.

Nora was exceedingly lucky in her team-mates, Honor Shorten who joined the staff in 1952 and developed a special interest in herbaceous plants, and Henry Guy, who first worked in the West Field under Rosemary Dobereiner and who gradually assumed the role of Shop Manager. It was from Honor that the writer had a first-hand account of a day at the shop with all its problems and satisfactions. The pattern of the day followed closely that of the wartime pioneers with its early start, the ice-cold marketing shed in winter, the need to get a move on with the final packing. The canvas-topped lorry, already crammed with vegetables, fruit bushes, apples, plants according to season and loaded the evening before, was driven round from its night in the barn for the flower boxes and pot plants to be jigsawed into the last available spaces — any overflow went into the little green van. Once at the market all had to be unloaded again on to a trolley and pushed to the shop site in relays before it could be arranged on the shelves, while all around the butchers, bakers and poultry men were equally busy. Each member of the Waterperry team was responsible for a particular section of the shop; Honor wrestled with trays and boxes of bedding plants or perennials, or with the colourful pot plants in winter, Nora presided over the fruit and cut flowers, Henry was the vegetable king. The edible goods were sold inside, while bushes and boxes containing soil stayed on the shelves outside.

This 'setting up' involving load after load of produce all to be displayed, priced and labelled as attractively as possible was quite exhausting, and it was no wonder that breakfast was as welcome in the post-war years as it had been before, a real breakfast of bacon, egg, tomato and sausage with buttered toast and cups of scalding tea designed to thaw frozen fingers. Any market is, by definition, a cold place and Oxford's is no exception, while Waterperry's particular spot on its splendid corner always seemed to attract more than its share of draughts. After breakfast the revived workers would usually find a reproachful queue waiting, wondering perhaps why the Waterperry staff needed to eat, and seldom giving a thought to when or how the produce arrived. From the moment the door was unlocked "all hell was let loose" to use Honor's description, especially at planting times. These were days before polythene packs, light containers and soilless composts; bedding plants, pricked out into soil-filled wooden boxes, had to be trowelled out, wrapped in newspaper and labelled, and the spare soil dealt with. Along with the plants went, if asked for, precious advice on how, when and where to plant, often the most satisfying part of the transaction since no grower likes to think of his or her progeny in danger of ill-treatment.

Good fresh produce and expertise were an irresistible combination to customers, and the shop soon built up a fine reputation. It also had a name for caring for individual needs, and much credit for this must go to Henry Guy, a hard-working man with a twinkle in the eye, a sunny disposition that made light of any problem, and the charm and ability to smooth the most difficult customer. He always made a point of looking after the less profitable clients and would select one carrot and one onion for an impoverished pensioner in a 'bed-sit' as carefully as he would pick out delicacies for the wives of College dons. Henry's 'old ladies' were legion and some refused to be served by anyone else behind the counter; nothing ruffled him, and he could find humour in the most unlikely situations. Ill-health eventually caused his retirement and he faced increasing breathlessness with the same quiet courage and humour until his death in 1983.

The students, neat in dungarees and white shirts in summer and green breeches in winter — which provoked cries of 'Horsey, horsey' from the market men in early morning — took their turns with the selling. The best memory for them all was the breakfast, probably more in one meal than in a week of breakfasts at Waterperry. Many enjoyed driving up the High at an hour when most of Oxford was still asleep, the freedom of finding their own lunch armed with a set amount of money from the takings, a snatched cup of tea in Hunts at the end of the day. For some, dealing with the public and the mechanics of selling was quite a challenge, and those who were not quick at mental arithmetic did not go very often. Honor Shorten was very adept at quietly taking over 'difficult' customers, and shielding diffident students. Some, like Janet Wood who had a good head for figures, considered shop days to be highlights in their training, and were delighted to be asked to fill in on extra occasions. There were no calculating tills to help them out, just a wooden box with a drawer and the old tin under the shelf for the final moneys.

As in the war years the variety of produce made the Waterperry Shop 'special', the exotic sounding vegetables, the freshly cut herbs, the soft fruit tenderly picked and beautifully presented. The era of tasteless commercial varieties was beginning, but customers were still aware that they had palates and that Royal Sovereign strawberries tasted unlike any others. The wide range of apples picked from the South Field cordons before the commercial orchard came into being helped to educate the public into the delights of Kings Acre Pippin, Orleans Reinette, Charles Ross and Egremont Russet. Always colourful, the shop was a positive riot at Christmas hung about with holly wreaths which spilled over on to their friend the butcher on the opposite side of the lane.

Sadly the Oxford shop could not survive the demise of the Horticultural School. The switch from an educational establishment with its student work force meant inevitable changes, while conditions in Oxford had become more and more difficult with increased rents, parking restrictions, and a one-way system which involved circling the centre before coming to rest in Market Street. With the opening up of the gardens to the public and the innovation of a tea-room it was decided reluctantly to abandon the City outlet and concentrate on Waterperry itself as the selling centre.

Chapter Eight

In 1947 Magdalen College decided to sell the Waterperry estate, and at last Beatrix Havergal and Avice Sanders had a chance to own the school they had created. Characteristically the decision to buy was reached slowly, and they had to have financial help. The then Bursar of Magdalen, Colin Cooke, spells out the situation clearly in his Letter of August 22nd, 1948.

> Your lease of Waterperry House and the land both expire at Michaelmas 1948. The land alone regarded separately from the House is a reasonable investment for the College, giving a reasonable return. The House and buildings which have a separate lease are however an investment which produces only an expense to the College. As I mentioned to you, our annual expenditure on repairs is much greater than the income we derive from the property. It would therefore be of advantage to the College to sell the House and buildings, and I believe it would be to the advantage of your Institution to consider acquiring the freehold, since it would then give you that security of tenure which will enable you to drive full benefit from the goodwill that you have built up. As a going concern Waterperry Horticultural School is dependent at present on the College's attitude with regard to your tenancy, and that attitude must necessarily be governed to a considerable extent by the return the College receives from the property. Both from your point of view and ours it is really necessary to come to a decision as soon as possible, in view of the expiry of your lease next year.

On 24th February, 1948, Miss Havergal was told by the agents, Carter Jonas and Sons, that the College agents were recommending to the College that they should sell her the house and sixty acres of land which she was renting for the sum of £8,250. The College, generous to the last, would pay its own costs, not the usual practice with College property, so saving her about £300. There was a possibility that she could buy more land at approximately £50 per acre, depending on the situation, and Carter Jonas suggested a definite offer to the College. On the 16th of March they were writing more urgently for a decision. 'The College have definitely decided to sell the property and if you do not wish to buy it they propose to offer it elsewhere. While we are certain the College would not want to sell it over your head we do feel that it is desirable that you should come to some decision as soon as possible.'

Decision making was difficult enough, raising money could have been more so. Not for the first time Downe House connections proved invaluable. A former Downe House pupil and friend, living in Oxford, arranged for a mortgage to secure sufficient funds at very low interest, a business agreement but a most generous gesture, and one that provided the final stimulus for success. This benefactress's brother had, as an undergraduate, been the very first customer for fruit from Pusey, so the association was well rooted. The Principals were now able to buy Waterperry and added land, bringing the whole up to the present eighty acres by adding seven to the West Field, and taking in the thirteen acre meadow below the South Field. In late 1948 the sale was approved by the Ministry of Agriculture and fisheries, who expressed themselves satisfied 'as to the propriety thereof' and on 28th January, 1949, the documents relating to the mortgage were signed and sealed. The Principals had come a long way from the gardeners' cottage at Pusey.

While Miss H. and Miss S. had worked incredibly hard and overcome many difficulties Providence did come to their aid at quite regular intervals, very much as booster rockets firing a space vehicle into higher orbit when the engine falters. The war was neither desired nor desirable but it came at the right time for Waterperry. Their benefactress provided the next 'lift' and there was still a fairy godmother waiting in the wings to provide one more. But one of the greatest factors in the Horticultural School's success was that by 1948, when they were able to own the estate, they had gathered a nucleus of outstanding young women on their staff who were equally dedicated to the success of the school. Many women can say, proudly, that they played some part in the enterprise, and former students will have specific memories of good teachers up to the closure. But the group who gathered in the years before the Magdalen sale set the definitive standards, and two of them were still there to guide the remnants in the difficult years after closure.

First of this group was Joan Stokes, already mentioned as a teenage student in 1934. When Beatrix Havergal accepted her, not without misgivings, she made one of her best investments, investment in loyalty, dedication and considerable skill. Joan, Stokey to her friends, was a tiny person with a severe spinal curvature; more importantly she had the courage and zest for living which overcame physical handicap. On meeting her one was only aware of her vivid and attractive face, radiant smile and her rich West Country voice. She was very much a personage in her own right, not in spite of her handicap but because of her innate ability. After her training Miss H. put her to work in the Alpine nursery, clearly with the idea of sparing her physically. Stokey felt cut down to size, and was unhappy until she could persuade Miss H. that this was not her rightful place. By 1936 she was listed as 'Foreman of the Glasshouses', a post she held all her working life. Her small kingdom at this time consisted of the conservatory with its orange tree and potting shed at its rear, the vinery and melon house adjoining it, and two other houses. One of these, no longer in existence, seemed made to measure for this particular foreman since any tall visitors invariably cracked their heads on the lintel.

From that time Stokey was in complete control, and presided over the gradual build-up of the department with the addition of several houses. Her most spectacular achievement was to produce the Royal Sovereign strawberry plants laden with ripe fruit at exactly the right moment to win fifteen Gold Medals at Chelsea Flower Show between 1955 and 1970. Miss H. was wholeheartedly and emotionally involved, wont to visit the glasshouses at midnight and write a frequently despairing diary while sitting on the water tank in the second house, but eternal credit must go to Joan Stokes who bore the day-to-day responsibility and managed to keep calm and reassuring. The writer was given an amusing and very apt description by the present Oxfordshire Horticultural Adviser, Tom Farrer, of his first sight of these two growers at Chelsea, Beatrix Havergal surging through the crowds in the vast exhibition tent, a path appearing miraculously before her and Joan Stokes trotting several yards behind in her 'wash'. Stokey's skill was recognized by the Royal Horticultural Society with the award of an Associateship of Honour in 1969. On that occasion the President told her that in the years she had been responsible for the difficult production and timing of the Chelsea plants no strawberry unworthy of the name of Royal Sovereign had ever found its way on to her stand. "Unless," said Lord Aberconway, "perhaps you have inserted such a one at the back to make its fellows blush scarlet with horror at the right moment."

The Chelsea Show was a major event in every year and deserves a chapter to itself; the day-to-day glasshouses under Stokey's rule were always a picture of order and horticultural know-how. The cucumber and tomato houses with their immaculate stringing and clean bright fruit were as attractive as the magnificent displays of primulas and cyclamen in the winter months. She had a personal success too with a Show display of the streptocarpus Constant Nymph in 1966. That great gardener, Margery Fish, wrote in *The Field*: 'The streptocarpus Constant Nymph is well known, but I had not realized how beautiful it is until I saw the displays of massed plants from Waterperry Horticultural School. These had been grown by Joan Stokes, proof of great skill.' Love of streptocarpus could be listed as a Waterperry trait over the years and still enduring, all due to the initiative — or light-fingeredness — of a student in the '46 group, Prudence Parsons. The group had been taken to the John Innes Research Station at Merton where the blue streptocarpus, Constant Nymph, was being developed. Prudence, with the connivance of one of the John Innes staff, 'acquired' a leaf, and bore it back wrapped in a wet handkerchief, the progenitor of many lovely displays in the future. Following John Innes' patronizing attitude to the 'girls training in practical gardening' this seems a fair example of spoiling the Egyptians.

Despite her lack of inches — round portions of tree trunk on which she needed to stand to reach the bench can still be seen in the potting shed — Stokey was tireless and pretty ruthless when necessary. An animal lover, usually with a little cat for company in the glasshouses, she nevertheless kept a mole stick in the early years, one notch added for each velvety victim. Less than enthusiastic students, such as those who tried to get away with half instead of whole barrow loads of soil mixture, were castigated severely, even more over transgressions when watering. In mitigation she had been known to leave a bottle of cider at the end of interminable frame ground paths to be hoed in the heat of a summer's day. But her word was law in her own department and the student who, feeling hospitable, actually gave a melon away, albeit to a member of the Henley family on a nostalgic visit, was never allowed to forget it; every fruit had been carefully counted. Joan Stokes was devoted to Miss H. but doubts have been expressed as to whether her influence on Miss H. was always helpful in student assessment. If Stokey took a dislike to a student, that student had a problem; since she liked girls who were assured and amusing and could make her laugh, some capable but shyer girls found themselves with more than their fair share of the drearier jobs, and with a negative or even adverse report. It is almost inevitable for there to be favourites in a small rather intense community, indeed Miss

H. was the worst offender in this respect, but a few careers may have been blighted as a result.

Away from her responsibilities Joan Stokes was game for anything, and her performance as a rumbustious Toad to Mary Spiller's Rat in a staff rendering of *The Wind in the Willows* is still remembered. The Principals bought her an Austin car to mark her first 25 years at Waterperry and she soon learnt to drive, taught by the always helpful taxi-man from Wheatley, Mr Walde. In later years she launched out on a new blue Mini, adapted to her needs, and would drive off for her Shropshire holidays perched up happily in the new toy, completely surrounded with plants for the new garden she was creating. During her time in Waterperry she played a great part in village and Church affairs, and was Secretary of the Parochial Church Council for twenty-one years, a splendid record; her Minutes of countless meetings read very like her, robust, efficient, without frills and with a certain lack of punctuation, and the same qualities spilled over into her letters which were always lengthy, personal, and funny. An extract from a letter written to Miss H. when the latter was on holiday gives a good idea of her style.

> I had a super lunch and got settled down in the warm, then poor Sue turned up at the window, got a woman who had come for a big apple order all put up for her on the table but she said the Blenheims were not Blenheims. So I have had to go out and deal with her, most extraordinary woman, wife of a don from Christchurch, the apples were Blenheims all right but fantastically beautifully coloured this year. Anyway I got round her, you would have laughed if you had heard her. I said "If you don't think they are Blenheims try one" but she said she had just had a huge lunch so I said, "well have one bite" so she did and said "Oh wonderful, you are quite right" and then gobbled up the complete apple. Then she said "How long do you think this lot will last me?" I felt like saying "Not long if you gobble them up at the rate you have just eaten that one" but I had to restrain myself and just say "Well, it just depends" and so she went on and in the end she decided to ring up and buy a lot of Coxes. She was dressed in a huge purple hat with scarf attached which came down round her ears and under her chin, black coat and high black boots what is more she let me load the lot and never even gave me a tip! There are some funny people about.

No doubt the 'extraordinary woman' found Stokey equally fascinating, and Waterperry has never been quite the same without her indomitable little figure.

Two years behind Joan Stokes, Josephine Cockin arrived as a student in the spring of 1936. Always known as Jo she was to have tremendous influence on the school, and it was due to her as much as anyone that the training was so successful. Coming from a well-to-do family and used to command, she was never intimidated by the Havergal manner, rather overwhelming to some, and was one of the few members of staff who really seem to have held their own ground if necessary. Small and wiry, she was extremely tough both physically and mentally, and so got on well with Miss S., no doubt on grounds of mutual respect as well as affection. The two women were very alike, somewhat sharp and prone to sarcasm while never suffering fools gladly, but towers of strength in times of need. Quick and caustic minds are often daunting to the young, and undoubtedly some students were much in awe of Jo Cockin. One well-known grower confessed that she still has a complete 'block' as regards pruning fruit as a result of Jo's strictures, and perhaps it was fortunate that she was destined to spend her days with herbaceous plants instead. Several former students remember being members of frozen semicircles round fruit trees or facing the kitchen garden wall, numb with cold and apprehensive of a difficult question while Jo, oblivious to weather conditions, held forth. There must be many who, like Ursula Ward, having painstakingly planted a long row of strawberry plants saw them ruthlessly pulled out again by Jo as not planted firmly enough.

But such incidents were relatively rare and very much in a good cause, neither should Jo Cockin be seen as in any way dour or forbidding. Certainly she knew her own mind, but it was a lively incisive one and helped to bring a little fresh air into what could be rather an intense atmosphere. She was not averse to breaking out as junior staff when, with Liz Stewart and Sheila Bellow, she climbed out of her bedroom window for a midnight row in the boat Piglet one beautiful moonlit night. It was to Jo Cockin that Waterperry owed the advent of the distinctive uniform, the green dungarees. The early uniform had been transferred from Thatcham, via Pusey, and was substantial to say the least. "How did we support our uniform?" wrote Mary Rowlatt of the Pusey days. They were allowed cotton breeches in summer in place of the heavy cords, but shirts were buttoned up to the neck underneath a smock overall, with thick knee stockings to complement the breeches, the whole topped with a hat. Things were little better at Waterperry until Jo and a brave accomplice presented themselves at Work Reading on a hot day wearing navy boiler suits, the sturdy garage mechanic type of garment with a metal clip over buttons on the bib. Doubtless there were ructions but they stood their ground, and eventually dungarees were the order of the day, not the crude navy but of a very distinctive green, instantly recognizable and a blessing in the summer months. Like all uniform garments they failed to find favour with everyone, and in the last few years were superseded by the ubiquitous and often ugly jeans, while one group celebrated the end of their training by performing a ritual dance on the roof of the house tearing up their dungarees, a feat in itself as they were remarkably hard wearing. Physical make-up did present problems, since tall girls found that the large sizes still lacked length but were enormous round the waist, while well-endowed girls were inclined to bulge out of the bib in front. All wore leather belts in an attempt, usually very successful, to appear shapely, and end of year photographs present a very neat, workmanlike and attractive appearance, all in green dungarees with white shirts. Dungarees for women have their drawbacks; nevertheless it is amusing to find that they have now become fashionable garments.

Waterperry owes more to Jo Cockin than mere sartorial improvements, though in the same context friends will remember the sound of her expensive leather-soled brogues as compared with the rubber soles of poorer colleagues. She is remembered more for her craftsmanship and technical expertise which she was able to pass on to others, principally as Head of the Fruit Department. She stayed for thirteen years and, in her last two years, was joined by a young Land Army girl, Jean Manger, who absorbed her teaching and stayed for forty years, finally becoming the first manager of the Horticultural Centre as it became.

In 1942 another Land Army trainee who was to make her mark at Waterperry joined the staff, at first helping Miss H. with other Land Army recruits and then teaching the Horticultural students in the expanses of the West Field. Rosemary Dobereiner, tall, slim, and invariably known as 'Dobber' was an entirely different character from Jo Cockin and just as effective. Coming from an Army background and from a family of four brothers she nevertheless had nothing of the sergeant-major approach. Gentle, sunny natured and exceptionally hard working she taught by example, passing on her knowledge of plants and their care in the kindest way possible. She was also a good comic actress, and happily played the fool at entertainments. Many students will remember her with her little Dexter cow, Holly, who distinguished herself by walking into the big hall of the house, round it and out again without being reprimanded by Miss S. Dobber was always the one who volunteered to walk Boxer, the carthorse, to be shod by the blacksmith in Tiddington. Animals certainly vied with plants for her affections, and this was her undoing as far as Waterperry was concerned. After twelve years on the staff she was wooed and won by Cecil Meredith who had come up from Ross-on-Wye to farm Townsend Farm at the end of Waterperry village. The wedding was a lively event judging by the photographs, with students forming a guard of honour with hoes and rakes outside the church, the bride a good head taller than her husband. After two years Rosemary and Cecil moved to Lincolnshire and founded a farming dynasty with a family of six.

Many former students will admit that, given a choice of departments, they would plump for working in the little Alpine nursery tucked behind the house by the kitchen where Valerie Finnis was in charge. Perhaps it was a soft option physically compared with the rigours of the West Field but Valerie Finnis herself ensured that it was an exciting department to be in. Volatile and amusing with a strong histrionic streak, and blessed with a remarkable memory and feeling for plants, she charmed the students as indeed she charmed Miss H. in whose eyes she could do no wrong. She was not interested in working for the National Diploma; instead she took lessons on photography from taxi-man Walde and became one of the finest plant photographers in the country, a skill which earned her the award of the Victoria Medal of Honour in 1975, while she has also tried her hand at abstract painting with some success. Alpines were her first love and, building on Peggy Fonge's early collection, she greatly increased the collection of saxifrages, winning medals at Chelsea. Miss H.'s obvious affection did not always endear V.F., as she was known, to her colleagues, a fact of which she was well aware and would frequently sign herself 'Finis, the end' on greetings cards. Frictions apart she was undoubtedly the most gifted of the group, and her family circumstances made it possible for her to travel extensively and collect plants, all of which added to the interest of the Waterperry nursery. Eventually she married Sir David Scott, one of the few amateur gardeners whose knowledge and love of plants could equal her own, and with whom she created an exciting garden at Boughton in Northamptonshire.

Only one member of staff is honoured by name in the Waterperry Gardens, and one who would have considered herself the least likely. If you walk down the path beside the lower half of the herbaceous border and keep left above the rock garden you will find Sebb's Corner, a small woodland area where the first Christmas roses and snowdrops can be found, a delightful unshowy garden with hidden treasures. Mary Ebbs was older than the general run of students in 1945, and the rather clumsy sounding Miss Ebbs was soon shortened to Sebbs. Small, slight and extremely hard working, she seems to embody the best and most abiding aspects of Waterperry, the knowledge of being part of God's creation and the inner peace that still pervades the garden in spite of changes. Mary was guide and mentor to all who caught her enthusiasms for plants and for music, and she introduced many students to the glories of choral singing and of concerts in college chapels. When she could snatch time from the general flower garden she set about clearing and planting this discreet and secluded patch which now bears her name.

These were the women who left an indelible mark on Waterperry but many can look back with equal pride at their achievements. Miss H., a reluctant paper administrator as we have seen, left no files or personnel records, and the only lists extant of those who joined her are in two battered notebooks containing a double page for each term, students on the right, staff on the left. The first entry is for Pusey in September, 1928, listing Annelise Reinhart and Diana Purcell, going on to the first half-dozen at Waterperry in the September of 1932. The 1939 page, headed Outbreak of War, is confused but lists about five regular students and three staff, together with the Land Army short-stayers; at the end of hostilities in the autumn of '45 there were 14 confirmed full-time students, four of whom stayed on as junior staff, and six senior staff. On the last page of this notebook, dated August 1951, there were twenty-two students and sixteen staff, most of whom were Waterperry trained. The staff to student ratio was extremely high but these were not academics, rather practical gardeners who worked with the students in their own departments. Their expertise and the small grouping led to a very high level of achievement. During its best years Waterperry was being run as a very efficient gentleman's residence fortunate enough to have a big labour force, and with the labour force paying for the privilege of working there. The students were, in effect, paying for their training and working for their keep; time saving expedients were not called for, so results by and large were spectacular. When in 1947 Isabel Connor who had been gardening all through the war and who was, in her own words, "very cynical about trained gardeners" came as a prospective student she knew at once that anyone responsible for Waterperry could teach her all she needed to know.

The process of becoming junior staff was rather tortuous and shrouded in uncertainty. It was usually fairly obvious at the end of the

Summer Term and Examination Time who had a chance of staying on, but it was not *de rigueur* to enquire, and Miss H. made up her mind at the latest possible minute; this left any disappointed souls in a state of limbo until they could find themselves jobs. Certainly until the fifties Waterperry had something of the air of a finishing school, ideal perhaps for the non-ambitious and those who wanted a cloistered and happy existence. Not that Waterperry students were not sought after; they were highly regarded, and indeed hopeful requests as to where one could be found still come after many years of closure. Many girls came from horticultural backgrounds and returned to nurserymen fathers, a few went into teaching though that involved further training. But it was up to them to map out their own futures without any organized assistance with careers.

Marriage was classed as wastage and as really unworthy of a Waterperry training. In her last term in 1954 Bridget Ross-Lowe told Miss H. that she was engaged, to be met with the horrified reaction, "But what about the garden?" From that moment Bridget's was considered a wasted life; she was allowed to help with the strawberries for Chelsea but not allowed on the stand at the Show — she had put her hand to the plough and looked back. But equally typically all was forgiven when Bridget brought her young children to Waterperry, and she remembers Miss H. as both delighted and embarrassed, flapping her arms in an attempt to amuse the little ones, and welcoming them all. The youngest of these children has herself embarked on a career in horticulture, surely a good return on the original investment.

Probably the best known Waterperry-trained gardeners at the time of writing are Pamela Schwerdt and Sybylle Kreutzberger who together control the destiny of Sissinghurst, perhaps the most fascinating and the most visited garden in England. Both had been on the staff at Waterperry and went to work at Sissinghurst for the last two years of Vita Sackville-West's life, continuing to run the garden under the National Trust. Vita referred to them as 'her treasures, so well trained' and in their careful hands Sissinghurst has retained its magic. Both were made Associates of Honour by the Royal Horticultural Society in 1980. For a time they were joined at Sissinghurst by Susan Dickinson, one of the last intake of 1969, and she is now making a name for herself in Mrs Merton's beautiful garden at the Old Rectory, Burghfield. Wendy Carlile with her husband David Bowie runs the nursery started by her father at Twyford, and Carliles' herbaceous plants are always to be found at Chelsea and provide a focal point for Waterperry gatherings. Jennifer Lamond with her husband Patrick Woods are important members of the team at Edinburgh Botanic Gardens, while Wong Wai Ching, a student in '61, must be one of the furthest representatives of the school as she works in the Parks Department in Malaysia. Nearer home Sheena Burt, now Sheena Crossley, is a presenter for Radio Wales' weekly gardening programme while lecturing and running short courses for would-be gardeners. The student who has attracted the widest audience must be Mary Spiller, former Manager of the Waterperry Horticultural Centre. She returned to Waterperry in 1962 and became responsible for the very popular Day Courses run for amateurs throughout the year. As a result of a visit to Waterperry by the BBC with Geoffrey Smith, Mary was invited to become a presenter on television's Gardener's World, and Waterperry staff had the pleasure of sharing her expertise on several programmes, always hoping that Waterperry would get a little 'plug' or that a Waterperry plant would get a moment of glory.

The aim of the Waterperry Horticultural School had been clearly set out by the Principals in the 1937 Prospectus and it never altered. 'It is the object of the school to provide the theoretical foundation, the practical knowledge of Horticulture, and the specialized skill required to make a first-class gardener.' This insistence on practical skill, allied to sufficient theory, came from Miss H. herself and became the linchpin of the Waterperry training. She was a craftsman *par excellence* and students found the techniques of pruning or planting easy to remember because they had watched her. Like all good teachers she was a bit of an actress, and not averse to a little 'hamming'; there is a strong theatrical streak in the Havergal family, sister Frances working with Educational Drama and nephew Giles managing the Citizens' Theatre in Glasgow. Students soon learnt to play up to this dramatic approach, and would leave one obvious piece of shrub or fruit tree unpruned so that Miss H. could stride up when on her rounds and triumphantly remove it. She was a lively and amusing demonstrator in those early days, sometimes unwittingly as when, sharpening her knife on an earthenware pot she announced to her class, "Of course I was brought up on a pot." One student still remembers her solo performance as a NAAS officer, pacing up and down gazing anxiously at the ground with a severe-virus-hunting look on her face. There was always laughter when she was about. Her sheer size and ebullient manner — 'all noise and blow' as someone described it — but with kind twinkling eyes behind the glasses made her both impressive and endearing, and most people were swept along with her enthusiasms. She carried weight in more senses than one; Eppy Urquart remembers trying to dig in frosty weather to no avail, only for Miss H. to take the spade, plant her formidable foot upon the tread, and slide it in as though cutting cake.

In 1939 Miss Havergal wrote an article on Careers taking as her subject Market Gardening for Women, and one sentence said it all. 'The only way to learn is to DO the actual work.' In 1970, the last complete year of the Horticultural School when her partner had died and closure was almost certain, she was still upholding this in an interview for the *Oxford Times*. 'About six years ago I went to hear the Labour Minister of Education and was told that colleges could not be economical unless they had a hundred students, and that it was not desirable to combine practice with theory. Teach them the theory, said the Minister, and let growers give them the practice. What a way to run a Horticultural School! I couldn't do it. We combine theory with practice and this is the thing we value above all.' This aspect of the Waterperry training was surely its most attractive feature, and seems to have been a source of pride to students looking back. Of course there were weaknesses. Some found that they were ill-equipped for the more commercial aspects of horticulture when they left, some useful but newer methods were treated with suspicion, and there were gaps that had to be filled elsewhere such as the principles of landscaping. Many wished they had been taught more about horticultural machinery since the school owned very little. But the accent on personal skills was rewarding and infectious; the second year students had responsibility for their juniors and so were watchful of their own standards, the staff had to be one standard higher. Marjorie Mimms entered in 1946, and one of her first jobs was earthing celery with Rosemary Dobereiner, a demanding task by any standards; until she saw the perfection of the work she had no idea that gardening was not just a job but also a craft. Even now she finds the smell of celery nostalgic. Students are remembered not just as friends but as owners of special gifts, such as Felicity Rebbeck the best digger of her day, and Pam Schwerdt who could never be caught out in a specimen test. And when time was not really important what better way to spend an afternoon than by a warm brick wall tying in peach shoots to make the most perfect fan-shape possible?

In spite of an impression that the Principals would like to have hand-picked students as they did staff — and indeed Miss H. was not above delaying acceptance hoping that 'someone better' would turn up — it was essential that they attracted as many as possible if their heads were to be kept above water financially. In the early fifties prices in general began to soar, and the cost of energy, wages, repairs and materials

Gardening at Thatcham

Marketing at Thatcham

Avice Saunders, second left, and Beatrix Havergal, second right, with three students

Students at Pusey 1931.

Waterperry House with the church of St Mary the Virgin

The herbaceous border in 1932 when the School took over

Joan Stokes

Beatrix Havergal

Kitchen garden, 1946; demonstration of the use of cloches

Digging the South Field in 1932. L to R; D. Ashworth, B. Levy, M. Jarvis, W. Haytor, B. H.

Waterperry shop in Oxford's covered market. L to R; Student, H. Williams, N. White, H. Guy
Photo — Apex Photographic Services

B. H. with Royal Sovereign plant

Gold Medal exhibit of apples, Royal Horticultural Society's Hall, 1953
Photo — J. E. Downward FIBP

B. H. with HRH Princess Margaret at Chelsea

Gold Medal exhibit of Royal Sovereign strawberries, 1961

Valerie Finnis right, with a student in the Alpine Nursery

Mowing the big lawn

Digging a Celery Trench in the South Field. Photo -Tom L. Blau

The morning break. Photo — Tom L. Blau

Rosemary Dobereiner and Judy Fletcher with the wheel hoe. Photo — Tom L. Blau

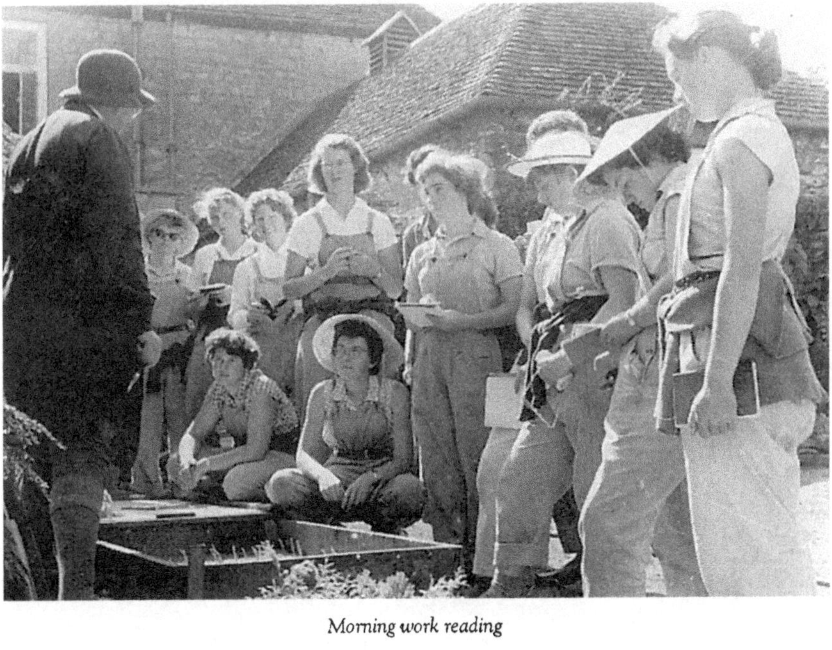

Morning work reading

View of the West Field

Order in the glass department — Joan Stokes's chrysanthemums

BH with Olive Willis of Downe House School

Group photograph 1957

Back row, Left to Right: E. Bishop, S. Norman-Butler, J. Upchurch, J. Burt, C. Moffat, B. Leneghan, J. Power, J. Williams, G. Dawson, A. Mountain

Standing: J. Macfarlane, T. Lansdowne, J. Bromley, J. Wood, J. Taylor, J. Nelson, P. Hicks, M. Sumner, A. Collins, S. Franklin, R. Castle, H. Collingwood-Selby

Sitting: H. Johns, L. Wasborough, J. Manger, A. Sanders, B. Havergal, N. White, J. Stokes, H. Shorten, C. Butler

On ground: H. Abbatt, F. Naismith, E. Gotto, R. Hyde, A. Carr, A Massee, P, Schwerdt, M. Moody-Stuart

Group photograph 1971

Back row, Left to Right: J. Foot, S. Fountain, P. Guy, C. Marland, Mrs Barker Benfield, S. Burnett, C. Halliday, F. Blake
Middle row: H. Collongwood-Selby with Polyantha, S. Hutton, S. Fable, J. Alexander, S. Dickinson, P. Fry, L. Beckett, A. Luty, K. Berry
Seated: M. Coe, J. Manger, Joan Stokes with Laddie, B. Havergal, M. Spiller, F. Brooke, S. Bedwell

Aerial view of the Horticultural School, 1959

all rose, affecting the school and prospective parents alike. At this time the grant system from Educational Authorities was in its infancy, and many local authorities were unwilling to contribute to training at privately run institutions. Only far-seeing parents would put their hands in their pockets when the State would help provide for what, on the face, seemed to be a similar training nearer home. Not all authorities were quite so blinkered, and Janet Wood, now Janet Lee, was fortunate with the Worcestershire Education Office in 1955. Her father had chosen Waterperry because it taught private methods as well as commercial and, a bonus in Mr Wood's eyes, it was for girls only so that there would be fewer distractions. Janet remembers little of the Waterperry interview apart from Miss H.'s striking appearance, but having been accepted by Waterperry she then had the ordeal of an interview by several people at the Worcestershire Education Office. At that time the Pershore Horticultural Institute had just been opened, and the Committee were justifiably proud of it. However Janet's father had primed her well with the essential arguments, citing private methods and the chance to obtain the National Diploma in the future. She got her grant, duly received her cheque at the beginning of each term and faithfully wrote her letter of thanks by return. But the problems remained for the school and Miss H.'s notebooks tell their own story. In 1955 and 1956 Waterperry was full with twenty-six students, one of whom had to be boarded out in the village. By 1958 they were down to sixteen, and an increase in fees proved insufficient and merely exacerbated the problem. In 1958 the Principals asked for an inspection by the Ministry of Education so that the school could be officially recognized, and Inspectors descended on Waterperry for three days in July, probing into every aspect of horticultural life.

Their report is almost entirely complimentary, and the staff in particular come out of the ordeal with flying colours. 'From the evidence to be seen, it is impossible to overstate the high efficiency and purpose of their work. All are very enthusiastic and hard working; they are able to handle students effectively and with a modest tolerance, and their craftsmanship is of a very high order.' Miss S.'s high standards, efficiency and inherent kindness are well noted; 'She has played an essential part in the whole development of the school.' Miss H. is seen as the leader, 'a strong positive personality tempered by a kind and genial disposition,' demanding high standards and firmly established as a national figure in the sphere of horticultural education. The organization comes in for considerable praise, the daily work reading which gave every student a sense of total involvement, and the responsibility given to Second Years to help and guide their juniors. Allocation of more than 50% of the training time to practical work is commended in a way that must have gladdened Miss H.'s heart. Commenting on the fact that, by the very nature of the work, lectures were given when opportunity presented itself — inspectors' jargon for bad weather — and so timetables not rigidly adhered to, they continue, 'Indeed it might be argued that the out-of-door theoretical instruction carries greater conviction by its direct application than many hours spent in a lecture room dealing with subject matter which, by its remoteness from the gardens is difficult of comprehension.' As Miss H. wrote more succinctly 'the only way to learn is to DO the work.'

One strong recommendation was made, that as soon as possible Waterperry should build a teaching block suitable for science teaching. The students needed more practical science, and the library obviously did not fill the bill. In 1958 that must have seemed like a pipe-dream, but at least the Principals had this excellent report, and the full recognition that they wanted. As always Miss H. turned to Olive Willis, mentor and guide, for approbation and advice, obviously with the money problem in mind. On 19th November Olive Willis wrote: 'It seems to me that this is not the moment to give way to any doubts and surmises — you are not likely to make a fortune but you have done what you set out to do, to make the best horticultural training in the world, and to relate this training to the spiritual as well as to the material world. There is really no alternative because you have taken up this work not as a money-making concern but as a vocation, and with your temperament and faith having put your hand to the plough you will not take it off until you are called away. Financially of course you have always been on a shoe-string, but what are shoe-strings for except to pull you through the hard way? Do not let your mind wander on these matters. This report opens new doors . . . . You can't count on Government support, always uncertain, but personal interviews will always achieve something. You must be an importunate, if patient widow.'

Chapter Nine

With Her Majesty's Inspectors satisfied and back at base, and with Waterperry officially recognized, Miss H. seems to have taken Olive Willis's advice and explored a few new avenues. Later in 1959 she was flirting with the County Education Committee, the Director at that time being Mr Chorlton, in an attempt to form an educational link and so to play some part in the training of teachers of gardening and rural science in the schools. The minutes of the Agricultural Education Board, meeting in November, report a discussion with Miss H. on the De la Warr report which commended rural science teaching of this sort. The minutes conclude that Miss H. would welcome opportunities for the Horticultural School to play a larger part in the training of teachers of gardening, especially at the secondary school stage when she felt that interest in the land might most profitably be encouraged. The Education Committee for its part was of no doubt that if a link could be made between Waterperry and the secondary schools on the lines of a pioneering experiment already in existence in Worcestershire there would be very considerable advantages. What was needed at Waterperry was some form of Lecture Room-cum-laboratory.

This desirable building, recognized by everyone to be essential and quite out of reach without assistance, seems to have been in the forefront of Miss H.'s mind, even through the triumphs of 1960. 23rd February, 1960 was indeed a Red Letter Day in the annals of Waterperry. In the morning Miss H., accompanied of course by Miss S., went to Buckingham Palace to receive the MBE from the Queen for her services to education in the field of horticulture and, in the afternoon, received the Veitch Memorial Gold medal for the same services at the Annual Meeting of the Royal Horticultural Society. Beatrix Havergal was a devoted Royalist and revelled in her annual meetings with the 'Royals' at Chelsea. Now her efforts had been rewarded by the fount of all honour, and I feel sure that Her Majesty enquired after those other Royal Sovereigns in passing.

The awards gave tremendous pleasure to students and former students alike and letters of congratulation came flooding in. Among them was one from Majorie Parry who had been one of the first students in 1937 and Miss H.'s reply is worth recording:

> I have been overwhelmed with letters and telegrams since January 1st, such nice letters . . . . The awards have come as a great surprise to me, and are tremendously encouraging to us all. I only wish everyone who has contributed to the building up of Waterperry either as staff or student could settle down to read the 300-odd lovely letters — you would then feel the glow and excitement and share in the honours.
>
> I am so grateful to everyone particularly the great stalwarts of the past! and you yourself played a splendid part. It is lovely to read what you wrote to the effect that you would not have missed your time here. For that I am truly thankful, for I live perpetually dissatisfied with this place as a training place for horticulture for I long for vast sums of capital to build the vital and much wanted buildings — and so I have lived ever since we came here.
>
> It is quite heartbreaking to see how easy it is for the Ministry of Agriculture to build places — vast sums, thousands and thousands are being spent and have been spent since the War on Conference Rooms looking like Ballrooms! Lecture rooms, laboratories, machinery instruction sheds — oh! wonderful places and we are all real Cinderellas — but it is wonderful to find that so many people praise our system of training . . . I loved our early years and the delightful pioneer spirit and courage of the staff and students of those days, and never shall I forget the hardships you were all faced with. How heroically you all endured them. Nowadays the students expect everything in the way of luxury! It is quite incredible but that spirit is everywhere.

In 1961, the year after these triumphs Miss H. attended a Horticultural Education Association Conference which affirmed the need for efficiency, certainly as much efficiency as that shown by foreigners, in the field of marketing, never a strong point with the British. The shortage of teachers was another problem and the Conference urged the Minister of Education, Sir David Eccles, to introduce a system of Courses in Horticulture available at all levels, and to establish Craft Training Centres for school leavers and day release students. The City and Guild examinations, designed to encourage higher standards of craftsmanship and improve qualifications had been in existence since 1878 but more was needed.

These official alarms about the need for more and better training and more teachers merely emphasized what Miss H. had been attempting to do ever since Pusey days. Apart from her own students Land Army girls had been taught during the war, and later there were the Open Days when the general public was allowed to look inside at what was very much a closed community. Nowadays when the gardens are open to all at any time of the day, and when summer weekends find cars streaming up the village to the car-parks it is sometimes difficult to recall the peace of those earlier days. There was great activity of course, and laughter and tensions, above all a sense of purpose but the place itself had an inner stillness. The discerning visitor to Waterperry still appreciates this unique atmosphere; only the noisy and the thoughtless miss it entirely. It was often possible to work in the South Field for hours on end without interruption of any kind; now only the West Field can provide that kind of refuge and even the West Field is divided from the Warren by the new Oxfordshire Way for walkers. The early Waterperry Open Days were then in some sense by invitation, and by implication only for those who wished to learn the mysteries of gardening. Sundays were ruled out almost entirely. The Sabbath was both remembered and kept holy, and only essential watering and ventilating carried out, the horticultural equivalent of loosing one's ox and ass; any livestock was cared for as usual. However straitened their circumstances the Principals would never have countenanced Sundays being treated as just another day in the week. Only Gardeners Sunday was allowed to be an exception when the gardens were open in aid of the Gardeners' Royal Benevolent Institution, but no demonstrations were set up as on the secular Open Days. In the programme of Open Days for 1958, the year of the Inspection, there were eight Saturdays when the gardens were open between 2 p.m. and 7 p.m. with a demonstration during the afternoon. That year visitors could have learnt about the care of seedlings in glasshouse and frames, seen the cultivation of early flowering chrysanthemum, watched propagation by taking cuttings, and found Miss H. at her favourite demonstration, the pruning of top or soft fruit, any of these for an entrance fee of 1/-. On one Saturday in July Waterperry took on a really festive aspect and was the venue for the annual Village Fête in aid of Village Hall Funds. Staff and students joined in with all the activities and students often showed off their skills in demonstration. Of course they reached only a small public but many amateurs were helped by this paving the way for more intensive amateur courses later.

'We are a real Cinderella' Miss H. had written to Marjorie Parry in 1960. Perhaps they were, but no one could have dared hope for a Fairy Godmother, such as the one who visited Waterperry in 1962. Miss Barbara Kitson, then living in Appleton House, was unknown to Miss H. but they had two assets in common, their passion for gardening and their helpful bank manager who watched over their two very different accounts. Knowing that Miss Kitson had had a financial windfall and was looking for someone or some institution needing help the manager arranged for her to visit Waterperry and meet Miss H. Over tea Miss H. doubtless waxed voluble over the need to develop courses, to hold lecture-demonstrations, and of her wish to be of much more use to groups like the Women's Institutes and amateurs in general. Before the afternoon was out Miss Kitson had, according to Waterperry folklore, offered to provide money for a lecture room extension.

This, by any standard, was a remarkable and generous action, and it is not very surprising that a legend grew up round the facts. According to the tale told very frequently by Miss H. herself she, overcome and flustered by this incredible offer from a hitherto unknown visitor, suggested that she must supply Miss Kitson with references from influential friends before anything definite was decided. While she was speaking — and those who knew Miss H. can well imagine her expression, joy and incredulity mixed — a robin flew into the room and perched happily on the back of Miss Kitson's chair. The robin, complete with worm, figured prominently in the Waterperry badge and proved in this instance to be a bird of considerable perspicacity. Miss Kitson was so impressed by this coincidence that she declared at once that the bird was sufficient reference for her.

It is a delightful story and the writer finds no difficulty in reconciling it with the fact that Barbara Kitson herself does not remember the incident. One feels that if a robin was not actually present it should have been. Indeed Miss Kitson is rather bird-like herself with her small spare frame and quick gestures together with an engaging habit of cocking her head slightly sideways the better to fix you with one bright eye. Perhaps Miss H. in a state of total euphoria confused the lady and the bird; the robin was a desirable extra and once Miss H. had a story fixed in her mind it seldom altered. What really mattered was the munificence of the gift and the joy it gave to both parties since Miss Kitson seems to have had as much pleasure and interest from her action as did Miss H. Miss H. never forgot her friends, kept Miss Kitson well in the picture and never failed to take the best of Joan Stokes's cyclamen to Appleton at Christmas.

Barbara Kitson's stipulation in 1962 was that her gift was to be kept anonymous as far as possible and very people in the past have known the identity of the Fairy Godmother. I have her permission now to quote from a couple of her letters which give a good idea of her directness and humour. On 16th May she wrote from Appleton House, confirming the famous tea-party decision while Miss H. had obviously sent along plans. 'To come straight to the point, I should like to make the School a gift in the form of shares in Ind Coope, Tetley Walker. Tetley and our family brewery recently amalgamated, and the take-over greatly increased my capital. People must drink enormous quantities of beer! I do not want it all, only makes for larger taxation.' There were to be no strings attached to the gift so as to give Miss H. a free hand but 'I'm sure the Demonstration Room will come first — would you perhaps consider something a little more comely than the designs you showed me?' She added that it was giving her much pleasure to have connections with Waterperry, 'much more fun to do it now than after I'm dead.' Something 'more comely' was submitted in the form of the low cedar wood building now so well known to Waterperry visitors and Miss Kitson, while finding it exciting, grieved over the two oak trees that had to be felled to make room. One more quotation from a later letter will suffice to show that she was a lady after Miss H's own heart. 'I am sending this (some form about money) back at once filled in to the best of my knowledge. So sorry I have no time to write a letter, it is so fine I must go out and anti-slug the delphiniums.'

At last Waterperry could have its Lecture rooms, the 'Lab Block' as it came to be known. The approach to the house took on an entirely new and much more open aspect as a result; not only had Miss Kitson's oaks to go but less lamentably the narrow cinder path between high dark box bushes which provided both access to the house and a right-of-way to the church, emerging by the yew tree. Students of a nervous disposition disliked this path intensely on dark nights. The account for clearing the site, dated 8th April, 1963 from the Wheatley firm of Powell and Son, also lists filling a pond area with material from a mound 75 yards away. The pond area, so-called, was not much more than a low lying wet area and barely duckworthy — the duck pond proper was on the other side of the path, now the site of a handsome Sales House. But the area needed to be filled and levelled. The filling material was a lucky by-product from the building of the A40 road, by-passing Wheatley. Miss H. happened to meet a trailer load of soil and, characteristically, stopped the driver and asked where he was going, to be told that it had to be dumped somewhere. So a long barrow-shaped mound appeared near the Abbey yard and was used to level the site. The trees were felled and either cut into stake lengths or logged for the house. Powells' £128 bill is made out to 'Miss Abergale', it being a curious fact that even after years of contacts, the names of both the Principals were found extraordinarily difficult by local folk. Women who worked at Waterperry for years pronounced Miss H. as Miss Have-a-gal which at least was apposite, while Avice Sanders was referred to almost invariably as Miss Saunders.

The prefabricated buildings, from Pratten and Co. of Midsomer Norton, seem to have gone up reasonably quickly and trouble free, though Miss H. indulged in a great deal of correspondence over the quality of blackboards and lighting and queried every costing. In September of '63 she was asking anxiously if the building could be finished by 1st November as she had found a VIP — unnamed — to open it. Obviously this was impossible as Joe Ashby of Waterstock put the final touches of paint and distemper in December. So it was the students of 63/64 who had the first real use of the rooms on their return from Christmas holidays, and the block soon assumed its air of permanence and of purposeful activity. In spite of the generous funding the architects did not get their settlement until much later. Their presumably final demand, which has survived, gives some inkling of the frustrations endured by many firms who did business with Miss H; the mounting fury expressed in one hundred-word sentence is really very funny — when viewed dispassionately and at a distance of time. 'Further to our letter on the 30th April last' — this particular letter dated 20th October 1965 — 'which you acknowledged on the 24th May that the Chelsea Flower Show necessitated your leaving the matter over until your return, and your postcard of the 13th September acknowledging the statement of account when it was noted that you were at present away on holiday and would write after your return at the end of the week the question of the outstanding balance due to this firm can no longer be delayed.'

It must be stressed that as with other overdue accounts, there was never the slightest intention to evade payment and, in this case, the money was there. But it does highlight Miss H.'s inherent inability to buckle down to less congenial tasks such as desk work. What began as a weakness almost amounted to a vice with increasing age and the loss of Avice Sanders's strong direction, and it spilled over into other school concerns, not just finance. Be that as it may, the architects' anguished letter was carefully preserved among her papers which indicates a clear conscience and a sense of humour.

The light, pleasant, three-room block, with cloakroom facilities at one end, made the most tremendous difference to staff and students alike, and it was sad that it came so late on in the school's life. One third was equipped as a simple but adequate laboratory, another as a demonstration room with bench space under the windows for individual practical work while seating a hundred people for lectures, while the central part could be used for social gatherings or extra lecture room as needed. Material for the students' classes no longer had to be hauled up the house stairs to the rather gloomy library, there to be cut up and examined on Miss S.'s precious library table, while basic skills such as seed sowing, pricking out and propagation could be acquired in warm comfortable conditions. Waterperry village benefited too, and the rooms were gratefully borrowed for Parish Meetings, harvest suppers and the Annual Fête.

Perhaps even more important the way was now clear to go forward from the Open Day demonstrations to begin Gardening Courses for amateurs. No longer would it be necessary for enthusiasts to be crammed into the icy marketing shed, sitting on boxes, window-sills, and even in the sink used for washing vegetables, while engrossed in Miss H.'s talks on pruning. In 1963, with this very much in mind, Mary Spiller returned to the Waterperry staff. She had been working as a free-lance fruit consultant in South Wales and Oxfordshire, and had considerable first-hand knowledge of the problems that beset amateur gardeners. She was now to be in charge of the Waterperry flower garden, teach the students and help Miss H. launch the new venture. Muriel Hodgman, the County Adviser for Horticulture, was fully involved from the beginning, and meetings between her and Miss H. to discuss content of courses and actual dates, were in full swing in October '63, well before the new building was finished.

It was decided to start with a Course in General Horticulture for the Oxfordshire Women's Institutes, and the suggested syllabus was circulated to all WIs. Rather startlingly 130 names came forward, and thirty of these were accepted, representing twenty Institutes. This enterprising group, who rejoiced in the name of the Guinea Pigs, stayed together for four years, having a day's tuition every month initially from March to November. They began with a general gardening course. In October of the same year a second general course was started and the Guinea Pigs added a Flower Course. Thereafter courses ran from October to June, there being the general and flower courses with either a fruit or a glasshouse course. The Guinea Pigs managed all four subjects and took their Proficiency Tests at the end, gaining excellent results from outside examiners.

In 1967 a Course for amateurs was started on Saturdays and this allowed gardeners of both sexes to attend. It was again a general Course and suitable subjects were chosen for the months available, October to December, March, April and June. By this time Day Release Courses for the young professional gardener were established at Waterperry, taught by staff of the County Agricultural Education Department but able to enjoy the facilities of the gardens; previously Day Release students had only conducted tours of the estate.

The amateur classes, which still flourish under Mary Spiller's sole direction, were most carefully organized. Initially Miss H. and Mary would spend the previous day preparing, working out the amount to be covered in great detail and listing all the necessary material. It was then Mary's responsibility to gather up all that was required. The same scheme held good for the amateurs as for the students, half theory and half practice; during the first half they watched and listened and noted, all now sitting comfortably — then they went out to put theory into practice. They were large classes and Miss H. and Mary divided them into two for the practical work, urging their own on to outdo the other.

A great deal of 'camaraderie' built up among the class members, and some displayed considerable fortitude in their pursuit of knowledge. One WI member attended her class the day before her baby was due, and insisted on seed sowing on hands and knees since, understandably, she could not bend far enough down. Another cheerfully abandoned her new baby to the care of whoever was providing refreshments and went off happily to her lectures; the baby seemed to thrive on such treatment. One could say that the Waterperry Garden Shop as we now have it was another infant product of those days. Joyce Moores provided the tea and coffee for class members on their arrival and also with their packed lunches, and she began to take orders for fruit and vegetables while setting up a little stall in the marketing shed. This was an innovation as all produce was still sold only in the Oxford market.

Waterperry has certainly gained a great many friends through these classes, and there is no doubt that a considerable amount of gardening knowledge has been spread abroad. The WI classes as such have declined in number so that the general public can have every chance, and the WI's new syllabus is now too comprehensive for proficiency tests to be feasible in the available time. But the public's interest in gardening matters seems insatiable and each year Mary Spiller, in co-operation with the present Horticultural Adviser to the County, Tom Farrar, initiates eager groups into the mysteries of growing. Rather sadly Miss Kitson's marvellous Lab Block has been transformed into a very pleasant tea room, providing welcome refreshment, not only to class members, but to the hundreds of visitors who come just to enjoy the gardens. The classes have a new home, a converted RAF hut tucked in under the Spinney, and the members can also practise their skills in the shelter of a polythene tunnel at the bottom of the South Field. The educational aspect is still strong at Waterperry, and the great-great-grandchildren of the original robin are still around to keep an eye on the practical side of things.

Splendid as the Lab Block was, another acquisition mainly provided by Miss Kitson probably did even more to improve the lot of the students and caused countless blessings to be invoked on her anonymous head. An immediate result of her 1962 visit, combining with a grant from the Ministry of Agriculture, was the installation of two rotund scarlet and black oil-fired boilers for the glasshouse heating, splendidly named Senior Robin Hoods. Students over the years who had battled underground with clinker, pink dust and the fear of Joan Stokes's displeasure, must have longed for this day. The two monsters were accommodated in their own house, just below the original below-stairs stokehole which was filled in, and they were provided with chimney, oil tank and, of course, liquid nourishment, always a very expensive item. Work in the glass department became, at a stroke, less anxious, less physical, and certainly less dirty, the two newcomers requiring little attention beyond daily checks on consumption of oil and water. At the time of writing the Robin Hoods still sit side by side in their dark little house, working well, if rather sadly, now that the Glass Department has lost much of its former glory.

Chapter Ten

Life as a Waterperry student was often uncomfortable, fraught with anxiety or full of frustration; it was seldom dull. A typical day taken from any term between the years of 1945 to 1970 would be full of happenings. It began early enough at 6.40 a.m. when a second-year student, a good riser, knocked firmly on every bedroom door. Twenty minutes were enough to dress, stagger down the back stairs to find a drink of tea and be outside to start work at 7 o'clock. The tea, for many, was more of an ordeal than an incentive. Miss S. left out thermos flasks brewed the night before, and the drink was milky, weak and often tepid; discerning tea-drinkers soon discovered which thermos was efficient, and made special efforts to be first at the long table outside the pantry.

At 7 o'clock all went to their allotted groups, changing round each week, and one set had to brave the mighty boilers which maintained the necessary heat in the glasshouses. Until 1962 these were coke fed and menacing. Their only merit, at least in winter, was that they provided a warm job, too warm for comfort at times, and more than one student bears scars from the radiating heat. It was an incredibly dirty assignment; and careful folk learnt to keep one old 'bra' in commission for boiler duty. The tools supplied for dealing with the monsters' entrails were heavy six-foot long pokers and required a certain amount of expertise. Ann Collins, a highly organized student who enjoyed a challenge, has left a clear account of the method to be employed. The poker was pushed along the bottom of the fire for its full length, then raised and lowered to heave up the contents, hopefully pushing clinker from the bottom up to the top where it could be raked away. If all was well done you were rewarded with a complete reflected glow on the floor under the fire; if there was any shadow the clinker had not been moved sufficiently and you risked the awesome possibilities of cold boilers and Joan Stokes's wrath. The stokeholes were well underground and the stokers were constantly needing to surface in order to clear their lungs of dust and fumes; supplies of coke had also to be barrowed down the holes as needed. Other members of this group noted temperatures in the houses and outside, ventilated if necessary and filled up water tanks for later use.

A second group, the West Field party, also had their anxious moments since they were on house duty and so had to face Miss S. The leader was responsible for seeing her the previous evening and finding out what vegetables were wanted in the house for the following day; some of the group then went out to the West Field to lift or pick that order, while the rest prepared vegetables already in for the day's meals. They also laid the breakfast tables, trying desperately to have all finished and correct before Miss S. appeared. Ann Collins who 'got on' with Miss S. made a careful list of everything to be done to ensure success, and this manual was much sought after by less organized leaders. Other early morning jobs included washing and crocking pots, cleaning and writing plant labels, making up seed boxes which was a favourite for anyone who fancied herself with a hammer, or sorting apples, a cold occupation requiring intense concentration. Rosemary McVitty remembers the horror of sorting rotting onions on a cold misty morning all alone as a very new student, and she soon learnt to line her wellington boots well with newspaper for extra insulation.

At 7.50 all went into the church, sang a hymn to Miss H.'s accompaniment, and joined in prayers led by her from the lower pulpit. The most welcome breakfast was at 8.10, usually consisting of porridge, bread and butter and marmalade, and something fried with fried bread. By 9.15 everyone, staff and students, was out in the frame ground for Miss H.'s work-reading, a vital part of the horticultural planning. The work force was divided into five groups, each containing first and second years with a leader, and these rotated round the departments, Glass, Flower Garden, Kitchen Garden with the South Field, Fruit and finally the West Field, spending a week in each. The daily report was therefore the vital centre of the whole concept. With a five-week rotation it was possible to miss working on a certain crop, and the work reading ensured that students had both a clear picture of their own task and knew exactly what was being done in other departments and could keep their invaluable diaries accordingly. The system obviously had to be flexible and at especially hectic times groups would combine; in impossible weather conditions they all met up for theory. Students also learnt to be wary of individual assignments. "I've just the job for you, so-and-so: you'll love doing this," often meant that Miss H. had some peculiarly unpleasant or uncomfortable job lined up. Needless to say work reading was not always a solemn affair; Miss H. laughed easily and she enjoyed practical jokes, those played on herself as much as any. Work readings on 1st April, All Fools Day, became a traditional time for japes to be played by either side. One year, when Miss H. had suffered several indignities before 9.15 she solemnly led the entire set into the boiler house on some pretext — and left them there. Another year an enterprising set hid one of their number behind the wall armed with a pile of broken glass and a large mallet. During work reading two others walked by ostentatiously carrying three expensive and precious frame lights. Once they were out of sight the concealed joker brought the mallet down on the broken glass, throwing Miss H. into a state of apprehension and alarm.

Tools were collected from the tool shed, each student having her own set of fork, spade, Dutch and draw hoe all marked with her number and hers to clean and oil at the end of the day. Individual tools were much treasured and, of course, improved with age and correct handling; they were the first and almost the saddest casualties of the eventual change of ownership. Work went on in departments with a welcome break for refreshment at 11 o'clock, when one student collected an elderly fish kettle from the kitchen containing bread and cheese or, later, rather dry buns, and took it round to all parties. Students in the middle years of the school would associate the 'lunch box' with Ben, Miss H.'s big black Labrador, a much loved member of the family. Ben was a glutton like all his breed and faced a dilemma every break time, uncertain whether to stay with the group first visited or to continue the round with the tin still full.

Midday found all the groups back at the glasshouses for watering. This was the great ritual of the day presided over by Joan Stokes, and was quite literally a matter of life and death since each plant was cared for as an individual. Ann Collins, caught running on one occasion between two lines of chrysanthemum in their twelve-inch pots, was told that if she fell and damaged one IT would go to hospital and SHE would be discarded on the compost heap. A graphic and amusing warning, but one that contained a grain of truth. Each student had certain plants to tend and water and plants have only one way of showing disapproval of bad treatment; they die. A dead or dying plant at Waterperry was considered to be a personal insult or a disgrace according to its keeper's temperament and, as importantly, in straitened circumstances every death was a loss. In large modern commercial premises where thousands of plants are reared, potted and fed by pressing buttons for automata deaths are part of the system and the dead are flung out as expendable.

Another excellent reason for such care was that every student was personally involved in success or failure. She was armed for watering with her own tapper, a stubby boxwood head whittled out by the handy Whitting and attached to a slender bamboo handle. Each earthenware pot — the ubiquitous plastics were not yet in vogue — was tapped on its side to determine the condition of the soil. A wet pot gave a dull sound, a dry one a clear ringing note. The waterer also had two cans, a small red one with a slender spout for the actual watering, and a large Hawes can from which to refill it, the large one in its turn being filled from the house tanks with water or liquid feed according to need. The whole operation with a full quota of students and well stocked houses was remarkably tuneful, but the tapper with the earthenware pot is seldom heard nowadays. Each student was also made responsible for a cucumber plant, the cucumber house as a whole presenting a most elegant spectacle with its intricate stringing and green pendulous fruit.

Lunch followed at one o'clock and was the main meal of the day, then came a respite until 2.15 when all went back to their departments. Fridays broke routine in that they were the days for specimen tests and for sprucing up the Flower Garden. For the tests Second Years took turns to collect pieces of shrub, flowers or weeds, to stick them in jam jars and challenge the rest to identify by both English and Latin names, an essential exercise for increasing plantsmanship. Friday lectures went on as usual but anyone available concentrated on applying spit and polish for the weekend, just in case Her Majesty the Queen decided to visit on the Saturday. She has not honoured Waterperry yet and visitors at that time were few and always by invitation, but the Flower Garden and all adjacent areas were always ready. Kipling would certainly have approved the use of broken dinner knives on the paths round the house. Ash paths were hoed and raked, lawns mown and swept and the edges cut, not a single Dutch light was allowed to stray out of its stack.

Five o'clock saw the ostensible end of the day though it was seldom so in fact. In the summer months staff went back to various chores after a cup of tea, students had their study for examinations to do and their work diaries to write up, while several had their own plots in the South Field and practised growing flowers and vegetables for their own satisfaction. A light cooked meal was provided at 7.30 and there were occasional evening lectures from visiting speakers. There was no official 'Lights out' but Miss S. was wont to look over her glasses at anyone suspected of burning expensive midnight oil and enquire coldly if the offender had fallen asleep over her books. The two Principals kept extraordinarily late hours. Miss H. frequently took the dog for its last walk at about midnight, while Miss S. was still busy in the kitchen keeping herself — and others — awake with an unmusical and monotonous humming. For most of the household the 6.40 knock on the door came all too soon.

This account of a typical day can only provide the bare bones of the activities; it gives little idea of the complexity of the work done, especially in the early years. A pile of ledgers provides detailed records of the day-to-day work loads in the 30s and 40s when one scribe kept an accurate and combined account for all departments. Later, as the departmental grouping became more clearly cut, staff heads of departments kept their own record so the overall picture was lost. Looking into the earlier records one is struck by the tremendous range of activity and the planning required if teaching programmes and production were both to be achieved. Not only did the students have to learn about crops; the crops themselves were essential in the constant battle to make both ends meet. Schedules had to take holidays into account, and indeed these seem curiously long for what was really a short period of training, no doubt they eased Miss S.'s task considerably. And there was always the weather to contend with, weather that could cancel a fortnight's work and put back essential sowing and planting with flood or drought.

Another aspect that comes over very clearly is the extreme care taken over every task, however small, and the far simpler materials used. Handwork was of course the order of the day; soil mixtures did not come pre-mixed and pre-packed in plastic bags, and each had to be prepared in accurate proportions. For example cyclamen were sown in a mixture made up of two parts loam, one part leaf mould with half parts of brick dust and sand, then pricked out into a second mix of two and a half parts loam, half a part of decayed manure, half of sand and brick dust with two ounces of lead arsenate against the dreaded vine weevil. The loam was Waterperry's great asset, but it all had to be dug out and barrowed, no light job, and chopped before use. Dried blood and bone figure largely in mixtures while peat, universally used in present day horticulture, is not mentioned in any ledger until 1945. It goes without saying that cultivation after ploughing was done by hand and that the hoe instead of weed killers kept weeds at bay. Chemicals were practically non-existent and only simple sprays used; in June 1935 for example we read that the black currants were sprayed with Quassie, one part to forty parts water combined with half a pound of soft soap to ten gallons of rain-water.

Digging was the basic skill and as such taken for granted. When Jean Manger arrived as a new Land Army girl in 1946 she was sent down to the South Field armed with a spade, and there she dug every day and all day for a week without a break. The South Field as a whole was dug each year, while the area round apple trees provided scope for real expertise. A perfect circle was forked round each tree so as to get rid of weed without damaging roots and the spaces between the circles were manured and dug, the worker attempting to leave the whole area weed free, fed and entirely level. The long lines of raspberry canes were treated in much the same way. A line was put down two feet from the canes and a gully cut along the line with a spade so that the workers could keep straight. The young canes had already been tied in and sprayed with tar oil; the two feet of soil either side was then forked and the long central space between the gullies dug. This was not purely for show though admittedly the finished area looked superb; the digging controlled cane suckers which inevitably come across and prevented any mixing of varieties. These were the fruiting beds; out in the West Field two acres of canes for selling also had to be forked, two feet on either side of each long line.

Elaborate and now almost forgotten methods were used to get quick and early vegetables and hot beds were made in front of several glass-houses. A five by four yard area was dug to ensure drainage and was then built up with layers of well turned straw and manure to a level of two feet, firmly pressed down and levelled. A French frame was placed on top, and more manure was banked round the outside to fill any spaces and conserve heat. When the bed reached a good temperature fourteen barrowloads of old potting soil created another six inches on top, and a final mixture of old potting soil, decayed manure, and sand raised the level to an inch above the framework. In three or four days the bed was ready for sowing. A light dressing of limed soil, half a pound per light, was raked in, and the whole surface firmed by laying boards across and walking on them. Two crops would often be sown, using alternate rows. Facing each other across the frame two workers would mark a drill by pulling the edge of a board ba.kwards and forward between them; the drill would be sown with carrots for example, and the second scored five inches away and sown with radish, then back to a carrot row. The seeds were lightly covered using the back of a rake, and the whole frame gently watered, covered with lights and then the additional matting for warmth and protection. Another bed might again be sown with radish, but also planted with lettuce started off in the houses for that purpose, two drills of radish and then a line of plants ten inches apart.

This was both heavy and meticulous work but it ensured early crops and so a head start over competitors. The raw material for this method was readily available from the stockyard but it had its perils. Rosemary Hyde remembers starting a new manure heap and rashly getting up on it, the better to fill her barrow. As a result she was covered in fleas and it was several days before she was again a respectable member of society. The livestock responsible, bullocks, pigs and hens, added to the work but also to the interest and the family atmosphere. No one seems to have developed much of a soft spot for the hens who appear to have developed every possible ailment. One batch was so bird-brained that Joan Stokes and a helper had to teach them how to perch, picking them up from the litter after dark and plonking them on their perches, only to see them topple off time and again on to the straw. In-pecking was another nasty habit, from food deficiency or boredom, and the victims had to be caught so that tar could be dabbed on the bare patches.

The pigs and the beef cattle, following on from the wartime stock, seem to have been much more popular quite apart from their side benefits, and, as part of the family, all had names. In 1948 a 'free' pig, obviously a runt thrown in with the purchase of six others, was called Eric, presumably to encourage his development. In the same year they fattened Hereford and Devon steers, and there was also a lady called Mrs Persil. In 1949 Sally, a sow, produced thirteen piglets and managed to rear eleven, while Emma and Erica produced twenty-four between them. Her Majesty's Inspectors in 1958 would have met the G class of porkers, Gavin, Gideon, Gervais, Gregory, and Gerald who, like Eric, came 'cheap' Since nothing at Waterperry was ever wasted the pigs were willing and ready to dispose of tired vegetables and unsaleable potatoes, unwittingly hastening their own ends.

This dislike of waste was not only concerned with produce, but was applied to time and, most importantly, space. The first apple trees planted in the West Field were placed well apart as was necessary for the strong root stocks then available. This was countered by planting blackcurrant bushes down the rows in the spaces between trees, and rhubarb was grown between the lines of trees. Modern spraying programmes would make this quite impossible today. The most intensive use of space was in the kitchen garden where glass cloches and span lights were used to produce early vegetables after the hot beds, a method which survived the change of ownership for a few years. The Kitchen Garden was certainly a grand sight when in full production with its straight rows of glass and meticulous spacing, double rows of barn cloches to the right and wider areas covered by French lights clamped into an inverted V on the left. These pairs of lights were no light weight and were carried between two workers to their positions on carefully measured bricks; it was a considerable help if the two were the same height and had the same length of stride. Never carry glass over glass was the unwritten law but one impossible to observe with the spans since the first pair had to set the line for the rest; they were therefore lifted over into the next space, the obstacle becoming longer and longer. Working with glass meant constant lifting and alteration. When the soil under the span had warmed sufficiently all were lifted off for the ground to be prepared, sown and watered, and then all lifted back. The next step was to space them as the crop needed to be hardened, which entailed moving two or three, changing the positions of the bricks and realigning the remaining spans. Gale force winds could blow them off their bricks and cause havoc, while even more unpleasantly an over-clamped pair of lights could crack across while being carried. The cloches were much easier to handle but often fell apart through, it would seem, sheer malice and contrariness. Nobody enjoyed cloche washing, a process involving a tank of very cold and eventually very dirty water and apparently resented as much by the cloches as by the operators. However the resulting stacks of shining glass were very satisfying.

Marketing the results of all this glass moving was the most satisfying of all. A year's harvest started under cloches would include lettuce, broad and runner bean, marrows, turnips, salad onions, peas, carrots, endive and dwarf French beans. Under the spans there could be several crops of radish, lettuce and carrot, and rows of all types of brassica plants for pulling and selling. Even after these crops the spans were used to make houses for outdoor tomatoes, by the simple expedient of adding two more lights to the original pair and bolting the structures together along the top. Tomatoes were planted underneath and the crops followed on after the ones raised in the warm houses. Gradually the cloches too were discarded and stacked, the runner beans stood tall and beautifully staked with long canes, while the marrows and courgettes spread themselves over the soil. The emphasis shifted to the later cropping in the South and West Fields and the Kitchen Garden waited for the next round of manuring, digging and covering.

The sheer volume of production was quite remarkable, and the work diaries seem weighed down by numbers. Seventeen thousand Royal Sovereign strawberry runners were pot layered in 1947 and the number crept up later to about twenty-five thousand, most of which were packed and sent off by post, this before postal charges became impossible. In

1946 nearly sixteen thousand blackcurrant hard wood cuttings were taken, and about three thousand gooseberries with the still familiar names of Careless, Keepsake and Whinham's Industry. Open ground strawberry runners came in their thousands to the marketing shed to be trimmed and sorted by a team of students and women from the village. The largest bundle of raspberry canes that could be sent away contained 500. The sorted canes were tied in twenty-fives, four of these into a hundred, then five hundreds together. Long wheatstraw was spread on the floor and then drawn up round the base of the bundle, the whole being wrapped in damp sacking and tied firmly round, more straw being put in up the sides. Vegetable output was equally impressive, a ton of cabbage being quite a usual wholesale order but the mind boggles at five tons of carrots loaded up for animal foodstuffs. While sowing was done with a small seed drill, easily pushed by the sower, a great deal of time was spent in the hairpin position, heads down and bottoms up, planting with trowels or dibbing in long rows of brassicas.

Obviously horticulture has altered in all its techniques and materials, even in its cultivars since the time of the school; it has not perhaps altered for the better, but it has changed and become, for many reasons, far less demanding physically. But the Waterperry students were fortunate in that they were not involved in the current attitude to time and clock-watching. Miss S. as we have seen, kept an orderly house with meals strictly to time, and woe betide the laggard who was late out at 7 a.m. But once the day was in motion the pressure of time was in some way removed. Fred Whitting had the right idea when he used to tell the novice diggers that they must first learn how to lean on their spades. The difference lay in the fact that the students were paying to work and to learn through that work, whereas the staff earned so little that money was of no importance and work satisfaction took over. Every day was filled with many many tasks but short cuts were neither necessary or desirable since they could seldom achieve perfection. Overtime was unrecognized and unknown, since time consisted solely for the work rather than for the work to be fitted into time.

Perhaps too the students were lucky to avoid the current restrictions and regulations regarding their personal safety. This remained their own responsibility, and all workers were expected to use their common sense; accidents, in short, were not expected. This seems entirely admirable, though perhaps one must criticize the Principals' total lack of concern about fire hazards. Out of doors the students soon learnt to avoid broken rungs of ladders, water the upper shelves in the glasshouses balancing on extremely rickety pairs of steps, clamber in and out of the granary without mishap and to survive the use of noxious materials, admittedly less lethal than present day mixtures, without the protection of space suits. Nowadays when it is actually illegal to ride on an open trolley with your feet dangling over the edge the onus to use your own wits is rather refreshing. In fact there was only one serious accident in the forty years of the school when a student was breaking up pots for crocking; a splinter went up into her face and she eventually lost an eye. Otherwise the main casualties were pulled muscles, strained backs and damaged fingers; not all sufferers can have shown the same restraint as Priscilla Prior who, having hit her own thumb full-bloodedly and painfully, remarked, "Bless me, how vexing!" to the huge delight of her fellow workers.

While the practical tasks led to the acquisition of horticultural skills it must not be forgotten that every student had a considerable amount of theory to absorb for examination. In two years, frequently punctuated by holidays, she had to acquire a large factual knowledge of such subjects as botany, plant physiology, mycology, entomology and the like, apply these to the varied departments of the garden and to the plant kingdom in general and be able to demonstrate the methods that were the outcome of such knowledge. A glance at a former student's notebook, lovingly preserved from the past, is certainly daunting. At least six lectures a week were fitted in to the programme, some of the sciences taken by an outside lecturer; later students remember with pleasure those given by John Paxton, Assistant Horticultural Adviser to the County and referred to affectionately as 'Packers' while Mary Thompson did sterling work with earlier years.

There is an idea, still current in certain circles, that those who work with their hands are invariably lacking in intellect. When the late Field Marshal Lord Wavell was a schoolboy at Winchester his headmaster had written, not very tactfully, to his father then a major-general, 'There is no need for your son to go into the Army; he is really quite intelligent,' an observation Lord Wavell used to quote with relish. The Waterperry students soon found that horticulture was no refuge for dull minds, and many had to work extremely hard to qualify. Miss H. had frequently to appeal to parents to encourage their daughters over this. 'It is essential to step up the thinking power of all the work that has to be done by hand,' she wrote to parents of a reluctant learner. 'Unfortunately students seldom realize how important the theory is until they reach their Second Year, and by that time they have so much to learn that there is not adequate time for the work.'

Happy the girls who could combine practical ability and physical skill with a good memory for fertilizers, cultivars, and the correct spacing for brassicas, who could instantly recall not only the name of a plant but its likely diseases and their possible cures. They needed sufficient knowledge to satisfy the examiners from the Royal Horticultural Society, answering papers for the Intermediate level of the National Diploma. At the same time they hoped to be awarded the Waterperry Diploma, and this had its own peculiar pitfalls. Not only must they satisfy the Waterperry staff in another set of papers and external assessors in a practical test, but they were also marked as to character. Each senior member of staff awarded marks for punctuality, willingness, reliability, and friendliness.

This unique system clearly had its weaknesses. One strained relationship with an influential member of staff could be as lethal as a black ball in a club ballot, and in such a closed community there was bound to be some friction. No present day college could or perhaps should operate on such lines. The obvious danger was that students might ingratiate themselves into good books and assume virtue while feeling decidedly unwilling and unfriendly; punctuality at least could not be faked. The remarkable fact remains that, on the whole, these dangers were avoided and the system worked. Olive Willis in 1942 had referred to Miss H.'s wish to create the finest of horticultural trainings and to relate it to spiritual aspects; the Principals were aiming to produce, not just good gardeners but helpful and reliable members of society. Obviously there were a few failures but over the years Waterperry girls stood out by reason of these attitudes in their work.

High ideals combined with somewhat ramshackle administration were endearing and infuriating aspects of the regime. The precious marks were seldom added up before the Second Years' last day at Waterperry, there was no formal Diploma presentation and, for many years, no actual written evidence of an award, a fact which was difficult to explain to prospective employers. Eventually a Diploma Certificate was printed but, as it had to be signed by an elusive Principal it could be weeks or months before the coveted card reached its owners. Frequently the owner, now in her first job, had to write once or twice begging for it to be sent, and eventually it would arrive with an apologetic letter from Miss H. pleading the usual pressures of work.

Miss H. increased her work load considerably by writing to the parents of every student at the end of her first year, commenting on her examination results and general progress. Every letter was written in longhand, and a carbon copy kept as record. On the one hand this process exemplified her very real interest in and concern for her girls. She wanted them to do their best, and she was also prepared to fight on their behalf if necessary. One County Council was implored not to remove a grant from a student who seemed likely to fail; the girl had a medical history and was slower than her contemporaries, but Miss H. was certain that she could succeed and was proved right. Another authority was asked to award an Agricultural Scholarship early so that a girl could enter Waterperry without the customary one year's experience; there was serious and prolonged illness in the family and Miss H. felt that the girl needed to get away from home, yet be in a family atmosphere. But the letter writing, even if frequently delayed, was perhaps Miss H.'s favourite way of making contacts. For all her apparent *bonhomie* one feels that she was not always at ease with students or parents. Certainly the individual interviews with students at the end of each term were rather traumatic and if a shy student was at a loss for words it shortened the interview considerably. More seriously it demonstrated her obsessive need to keep every detail in her own hands, and it was on this need that a continuing future for her school was to founder.

Chapter Eleven

The previous chapter would seem to indicate that Waterperry was a place requiring 'all work and no play', but I doubt if many of the Jills would have considered their lives dull. Obviously they had to be content with rather simpler ways of relaxation than the average student today. Oxford, for all the promise of the Prospectus, was quite distant when viewed from a bicycle or from an infrequent bus, and the 'intellectual society' of University life impinged very seldom on the early risers of Waterperry who had their own disciplines to master.

Students who wanted a really social life and some reasonable contacts with the opposite sex were at some disadvantage. "Men," as Miss H. frequently observed to Henry Guy, "were a necessary evil," and certainly treated as slightly below the salt. Although men were employed at Waterperry as lorry drivers, ploughmen, and for the heaviest of the land work only one was allowed to figure in the official photograph taken at the end of each year. Lieutenant-Commander Harry Collingwood-Selby RN who had married Miss H.'s sister, Frances, joined the staff in 1955, having survived a Japanese prison camp, and proved himself invaluable mowing lawns, driving the lorry, and as a handyman like most sailors. Invariably accompanied by Polly, his Yorkshire terrier sartorially correct with red-ribboned topknot, the 'Comm' as he was known was Havergal-in-law and so entitled to join the other staff in the photograph. This was to everyone's satisfaction as he was universally popular.

The one official meeting of the sexes favoured by the Principals was an annual invitation to the embryo curates of Cuddesdon Theological College the other side of Wheatley, irreverently nicknamed the 'Cuddlesdons' by the students. A posse of these gentlemen would be fetched in the shop lorry, all sitting precariously on bushel boxes in the back, and a rather giggly but usually decorous party was held. In 1954 the date chosen happened to be Hallowe'en, a night when anything was possible. In the event the men were taken on a ghost walk round the garden in the dark while the students tried to curdle their blood with various horrors. Jenny Lamond was discovered apparently hanging on a gallows from the granary, while Sally Maclagen was hidden up in the copper beech tree dropping wet sponges on their unsuspecting heads. In the excitement of the evening she was forgotten when the walk was over and her despairing cries were heard much later and her ladder returned. These very harmless meetings had the blessing of Kenneth Riches, then Principal of Cuddesdon and a good friend of Waterperry; his successor, Robert Runcie, put an end to such frolics.

Obviously such organized and strictly vetted events did not appeal to the freer spirits and considerable ingenuity was needed to overcome difficulties. One of the '61 intake used to meet her future husband in Oxford at weekends, staying with mutual friends, and he would drive her out from Oxford late in the evening to sign in, and then slip out again. One evening Patrick, the suitor, was sitting in his car parked discreetly in the yard waiting for his lady to return when Miss H. let out the dog. Hearing it Patrick leapt out and shinned up the yew tree; it was bright moonlight and the dog, rather like the hosts of Midian, prowled and prowled around, while the student did not dare leave the house. After what seemed eternity they met up at the car again and pushed it all the way to the gate before daring to start the engine. At seven next morning she was back to join the work groups. Other students locked out at 11 p m. found themselves spending what was left of the night on straw in the loft above the marketing shed; the dahlia tubers kept there over winter were, by common consent, voted to be extremely knobbly. Few accomplices would have dared to open the outside door for stragglers, but there was a well tried entry through a back window near the kitchen for some braver spirits.

Needless to say male visitors were not encouraged in the house, though during the sixties a great concession was made to allow the girls to entertain in a small room near the library. However terms were short and no one was deprived of male society for any great length of time. Since the only student to distinguish herself by walking out of the Royal Horticultural Society Examination was a young lady renowned for the number of telephone calls she received from admirers it would seem that the rather rigid attitude had some point. But the later and more emancipated intakes did find the air of disapproval rather irritating; it was hard to live in a boarding-school atmosphere at seventeen when you had already been given a latch key at home. One set made what they hoped would be a meaningful protest by painting out the school signpost at the corner on the Worminghall road and replacing it with Girls Available, but heavy rain spoiled the effect of their final fling.

Left to themselves the girls had to seek out their own entertainment. Theatre or picture going involved quite an effort, cycling to Wheatley to leave the bicycle at George's Café on the Triangle and bussing or hitch-hiking into Oxford, with a return journey in reverse. One group cycled the whole way in a downpour to see *The Mikado* at the Playhouse; luckily they were in the back row of the stalls and could hang their soaking wet stockings over the rail behind them. Back at the house they could play table-tennis in the ballroom-cum-common-room and there was a superb piano for the musical who wished to play. In the 1950s Waterperry village still had a hall and managed a monthly meeting, while the Committee managing the building was a judicious mixture of village and house. In 1952 for example the Chairman was Commander Pears, brother of Peter Pears, with Miss H. as Secretary, along with familiar names of Ted Fonge, John Guy, Cecil Meredith, Pat and Tom Owen and Fred Whitting. These were joined by Joan Stokes, Hilda Johns and Bindy Wasborough from the house. That winter's programme was varied and typical:

Oct. 17th Films — Birds — Herring — Heathrow.
Nov. 21st Illustrated travel talk.
Dec. 12th Christmas evening; talk followed by music with handbells.
Jan. 23rd General Knowledge Quiz — Waterperry v Garsington.
Feb. 20th I knew a great Man — talk by M. Deneke.
Mar. 20th Competition evening, Village v House.

There was also folk-dancing on Monday evenings from 7.30 to 10 when stamina must have been at a premium, and enthusiasts could also join in dancing at Tiddington and a little further afield at Culham College. In Coronation Year, 1953 however Miss S. hired a television set so that everyone could watch the ceremony. This was placed in the small hall at the bottom of the main staircase, together with two easy chairs for the Principals, and the students could sit in tiers on the stairs. The ceremony was, as we all know, magical and, as happened in so many houses, the 'telly' stayed. The students had an alternative home-based entertainment and this led to the rapid demise of the village hall evenings and the abandonment of the building itself.

One popular annual event linking house and village was the Christmas Party for the Waterperry children, and here Miss S. was the ruling spirit. She had always made it her business to know everyone in the village, kept a list of the children and their ages and saw to it that each had a suitable present to take home. The students decorated the rooms and organized games, no doubt in high spirits before going home themselves, and could occasionally manage special effects as when Santa, in the person of Jane Denny, arrived at the front door on his own horse with bells jingling. This splendid tradition is still carried on by the present house dwellers though the sophisticated young of today are more likely to be swept off to the Oxford Ice Rink rather than play games of French and English in the hall. In the same way students had fewer contacts with the village as the years went by, the students becoming more mobile and less content with simple pleasures and the village folk just as eager to look further afield. But many families were — and still are — closely connected with the day to day running of the house and gardens. Several of the Thomas family which came up from Wales with the Merediths helped in the house and with marketing, the gardens have benefited from three generations of Slaters while Cobb, Joiner and Clifford are all names linked with the school's history. One village institution that was always in favour was the village shop which did a roaring trade and supplemented the house diet, not always to the students' liking. In the early days it was owned by Millie Biggs, then finally by Wilfred Hassell, a most kindly man and a pillar of Waterperry Church. At his retirement the shop and post office ceased to be and inhabitants must go all the way to Wheatley to buy a stamp.

The seventh of July, Miss H.'s birthday, was an annual celebration for the house, perhaps not rating highly as a social event but a good excuse for an outing and remembered by many as a very happy day. Invariably celebrations took the form of a picnic and everyone bundled into the van or lorry, sitting on boxes and ready to be fortified with a splendid tea the better to sing lustily all the way back. The White Horse Hill was a favourite venue; in '46 there seems to have been a special celebration, perhaps to mark the first year of peace, and they all went to Stratford, had their party by the river and went to the Theatre afterwards. In 1955 the party went to Pusey, surely a nostalgic return for the Principals; less memorably they had a puncture on the way back. Whiteleaf Cross was another favourite spot, and the Sixtieth was at Burnham Beeches.

Any milestone in the annals was naturally an excuse for a party. In 1953 benefactors, friends including Miss Willis, staff and students gathered to celebrate the school's twenty-first birthday in style, the after-dinner speakers being Peggy Fonge née Chaplin, Muriel Hodgeman,

Bishop Riches translated from the care of the Cuddlesdons to Lincoln, and Beatrix Havergal herself. The last and greatest excuse came in 1966 to celebrate Miss H.'s award of the Victorian Medal of Honour from the Royal Horticultural Society.

Summer leisure time in the country needs little organizing and there was tennis, rowing on the river and illicit sunbathing, bare flesh being considered rather common by Miss S. The 66/67 group, a lively set considered rather rebellious for wanting to go out on Saturdays used to sunbathe on the roof, an out-of-bounds area but one which afforded complete privacy. A trail of chalk marks guided them through the labyrinth of rafters to reach the top. The same group renovated the old rowing boat, much in need of attention and rechristened it *Phred Bayr*, much to Joan Stokes's annoyance. Theirs was the only set to organize, not just mild rebellion, but riot, the great Cucumber Riot of 1967. This was a Demonstration by the Second Years to call attention to the fact that all was not well with their preparation of exams. These were getting near and the subject of cucumbers had not been covered. A cucumber somewhat larger than life was made out of an old green inflatable canoe, dressed in oilskins. At Work Reading the procession, preceded by the solemn tolling of the large handbell, marched to confront the staff with placards bearing the legends 'Cucumber Crisis — a lack of principal' (a telling thrust, as Miss H. gave the vegetable lectures), 'Take your Cue from this', 'Get to work on a cucumber', 'Ignorance is not bliss' and so on. It was a good rag but voiced the real anxiety being felt that Miss H. was past her best as a lecturer. Another real joke with no serious intent at all was played on Miss H. by Joan Horner, a Lancashire student. She rang from a local telephone box and, putting on a 'County' accent, declared that she had an empty piece of ground on her estate and that she wished to order one hundred banana plants to fill it. The students, hidden with bated breath on the stairs, heard Miss H.'s resounding voice exclaiming, "A hundred what?"

Hard work and simple pleasures were the students' lot and most of them found all they needed to be happy. During the last decade there were more grumbles, and more chafing at restrictions, inevitable as the Principals expected the post-war generations to have the same attitudes and sheltered upbringings as the majority of their prewar girls. The eighteen-year-olds in the sixties were more assured, brasher, and used to more comfort in their homes, and there was friction. Yet the Cucumber Rioters are the only set to have organized an annual reunion at Waterperry, a gathering now augmented by husbands and families, and there must be more to it than just wishing to revisit the scene of the crime.

Country dwellers usually consider that many moments of leisure are incomplete without animals, and the succession of Waterperry dogs certainly deserves mention. Ben, the black Labrador who followed James, the pioneer Sealyham, has already been mentioned as a glutton. He was also a canine Don Juan and spent much time courting in the village; he would return from these jaunts by slinking up the ha-ha separating the Warren from the West Field and then trotting in from the West Field gate with the air of one who has just put in a hard day's work in horticulture. A less endearing habit of his was to remove anything from a clothes line that took his fancy, pegs and all, and objects such as brooms and door mats also disappeared. Ever the showman, Ben had a funeral worthy of his talents. He lies six feet down under the beech tree wrapped in an old jacket of Miss H.'s, and the undertakers, Henry Guy and a German helper, had to work through thunder, dramatic lightning and torrential rain. To add to their problems the body was completely rigid by the time they were ready.

After Ben came Bruce, a fine golden retriever with a very different nature, not one to be trifled with. With the ingratitude of his kind he ignored Miss S. who invariably fed him, but adored Miss H. and would stand guard menacingly over her gloves or secateurs. At one time he was closely guarding the church as well, to the discomfiture of the incumbent, Mr Gillott. The reverend gentleman was no Saint Francis, and was moved to write to Miss H. expressing his alarm, apparently not finding the courage to beard the lady — or her lion — in her den. He complains 'Bruce persistently and increasingly meets me with intense aggression. You will, I think, not dispute the right of parson and people to approach and leave a parish church "without let or hindrance". I am told that it is unlikely that Bruce would bite. I do not hold that opinion and am not prepared willingly to take such risks as I have done to give him the benefit of the doubt. I have, of course, tried to make friends with the dog and do not enjoy admitting failure. I am prepared, if unmolested, to ignore him. I very much do not wish to hurt, or report him elsewhere. Will you please do anything you feel you can to allow me peaceful ingress to and egress from the Church to which you give such faithful service?' The rather pompous gentleman can have found little comfort in Miss H.'s reply; she writes that Bruce's aggression is 'an extraordinary thing, because he is perfectly friendly with all others and also tradesmen and even the new postman told me that he is no trouble whatever to him.' She suggests that the offering of a biscuit might be a solution.

We must have some sympathy for the nervous Gillott since Bruce was of very uncertain temper. Mr Grain, the 'Clock Man' apparently never allowed himself to be deterred but he may have resorted to bribery rather than suffer a break in routine. Clearly a calculating dog, Bruce enjoyed lurking in a large bush of Senecio greyii under the office window on Friday afternoons, ready to intimidate members of staff coming to collect legitimate wage packets. He was a wicked old dog in his way but was mourned at his death like the others, and was buried in the Warren with full honours.

Miss H., who could never be without a dog for long, then went to the local Animal Sanctuary to see a small white animal, similar to James, which had been recommended. She returned with Laddie, a large lolloping black retriever-cross who had captured her heart by bounding up and placing his paws on her shoulders, making it perfectly clear that she was his first choice. Very few could have withstood the appeal in Laddie's brown eyes, and he became a universal favourite. Joan Stokes loved him dearly and hoped to take him home with her after Miss H.'s death, but her sister was no dog lover. In the event he ended his days happily with Joan and Peter Bartlett in their cottage near Henley.

Leisure and Sundays used to be synonymous and, as we have already seen, the Principals only broke the third Commandment for essential duties. The little Church of St Mary the Virgin, tucked in between the house and the marketing yard played a very central role in the life of the community. The daily prayers were important, the Sunday services and care of the church an essential part of their existence.

Church and house at Waterperry have been, until recently, quite indivisible. Only two memorials in the church, both relating to priests, commemorate anyone other than house dwellers. The Warrior, Robert Fitz Elys, rigid in his stony armour, lived in a different house to the present one but it was on the same site. High up the Chancel hang the shields of Fitz Elys, Curson, and Henley together with that of Magdalen college, the school's first landlords. So although the ladies from Pusey set Waterperry on quite a new course and no doubt caused a stir they themselves were quickly absorbed into a church that had seen comings and goings for many centuries and remained the peaceful centre of it all. It is a remarkable church, not only for its treasures but for its unique atmosphere which manages to remain both holy and homely, a place, in Eliot's phrase, where 'prayer has been valid'. The Principals, both women of deep religious conviction, became in their turn its guardians and servants as Cursons and Henleys had been before them.

They were lucky in their first Vicar, John Todd, a man who served Waterperry for twenty-seven years and, to quote his memorial tablet, to whose loving care and eager research the church revealed its hidden treasures. John Todd was also Rector of Waterstock and lived in that parish where it is said that he was frequently at loggerheads with another formidable chatelaine, Miss Ashhurst of Waterstock House. Quiet and scholarly, yet determined, he was not to be intimidated by the gentry and it was rumoured that a china pig on his mantelpiece was christened Gertrude after his patron. His legacy to Waterperry was priceless; not only did he unearth the history of the church but he left a vivid record of his findings. These were gathered into a substantial and extremely readable guide book, published after his death and still delighting the many visitors who wish to learn more about the church and its treasures. It was John Todd who first uncovered the Saxon arch which curves high up over the pointed Norman arch to the Chancel. For years there was a board above the lower arch on which was painted the Ten Commandments and the Royal Arms of 1757. Instinct and knowledge gave him to suppose that there was an earlier arch and removal of both board and plaster proved him right. His grave can be found just outside the south door of the church.

Sunday by Sunday Miss H. and Miss S. would be found at services, going up together to their accustomed place at the altar rail for Communion, while Miss H. was often at the harmonium for other occasions. She was not the only accomplished player in the early days, Peggy Chaplin and Mary Ebbs of Sebbs Corner taking their turn at the pedals. This rather ramshackle instrument had the great merit in winter of keeping the player warm with the effort of supplying the necessary air. Fred Whitting also played a great part in improving the lot of the congregation, tending a round cast-iron boiler of the Tortoise type which he lit every morning during the winter months. Fred was a devoted member of the Church Council and the iron gates leading into the churchyard from the marketing yard were erected in his memory in 1973. Mrs Whitting played her part in looking after the altar linen, laundering and mending.

Miss H. soon added the office of churchwarden to her position as organist, an office she held until 1973. Waterperry has a tradition of long serving wardens, and Miss H.'s opposite number, Ted Fonge, held the post of Vicar's warden for 41 years before retiring at his own request. He is still first to arrive in order to warm the church for early services. Miss H.'s fine voice was another asset, giving the often small congregation confidence. Miss S., as would be expected, took a quieter role. Flowers were provided from the gardens and were arranged by her every week, while staff and students together helped to decorate the building for festivals. This virtual monopoly by the school was not entirely good for the parish and Waterperry villagers, whose church it was, were definitely discouraged from helping and from arranging their own gifts, a state of affairs that took many years to alter when the school closed.

John Todd died in 1952 and his successor was not popular; it is always difficult to follow a well loved village parson and the new appointment was doomed to failure. When the living was again vacant in 1960 it was decided to sever the link with Waterstock and Waterperry was joined with the village of Holton instead. There was never any doubt about the popularity of the first priest-in-charge of the new pairing. Canon Griffiths was much loved and several students remember the sad day in 1965 when he collapsed and died entering his church at Holton to take part in a choir practice. The next Vicar, Russell Hawken, launched into a much needed Restoration programme for St Mary the Virgin, and the school and village together threw themselves into money raising, encouraged by generous help from such bodies as the Friends of Oxfordshire Churches, and the Historic Churches Preservation Trust. Photographs and records of the immense amount of work needed, both outside and inside the building, can be seen in the display cabinet in the Lord's Aisle the cabinet itself a beautiful example of craftsmanship by Mr Harris in memory of his son, David, who had helped him restore the pulpit and box pews. It is poignant that in such a small church there are three memorials to young men of promise. The commemorative brass remembering a Midshipman Henley drowned at sea looks over to the table given in memory of Stephen Collingwood-Selby, another sailor's son and Miss H.'s nephew who died at the age of 25.

Russell Hawken retired to join his family in Australia leaving a beautifully restored church and another priceless treasure in a new stained glass window just inside the west door. Designed by King of Norwich it is an example of the very best twentieth century glass and incorporates many features associated with Waterperry past and present. Two roundels display a deer, still to be found in Waterperry wood, and a stylized pear tree by a brook, a play on the old name Periun, a collection of pear trees; these are linked by the words of the psalm, 'Like as the hart desireth the water-brooks, so longeth my soul after Thee, O God.' The delicate quarries surrounding the roundels display representative plants, the rose and the lily for the Virgin, mimosa and wattle for the donors' future home, and the Royal Sovereign strawberry for the Horticultural

School. The date of the gift, 1971, and the initials of Russell and Mary Hawken appear on the upper light. The task of restoring the medieval glass fell to Russell Hawken's successor, David Wood-Robinson, together with a complete re-slating of the chancel roof and, at the time of writing, the church is probably in better condition that it has been for many years. David Wood-Robinson, himself a keen gardener, is cousin to Ann Wood-Robinson, a former student, and so can fairly be said to be a school member by adoption. The benefice is now widened yet again to take in Tiddington with Albury, additions to the burdens of Holton, Waterperry and Waterstock.

Miss S.'s place near the door, as near as possible to her kitchen and close to the Waterperry window, is now marked by a memorial tablet, 'Remember Avice Josephine Sanders' Miss H. also presented the church with a Hammond electric organ in her memory, a splendid little instrument and a vast improvement on the old harmonium though it no longer has the merit of keeping the organist warm. Miss H.'s own memorial in one sense is all around the church in the gardens, but a formal tablet is to be erected in the building. The friends are buried together on the north side of the churchyard. Miss H.'s office of churchwarden passed, most suitably, to Jean Manger, who, by her devotion to Waterperry and sheer hard work, made the difficult transition from Horticultural School to Horticultural Centre a possibility. It is sad that after so many centuries church and house are no longer strongly linked in faith and worship.

Chapter Twelve

"And do you still show those beautiful strawberries at Chelsea?" is a perennial question asked of the present staff in Waterperry Garden Shop. Amateur and professional gardeners alike, if of a certain vintage, even if rather vague as to the Horticultural School and its work, invariably remember that the names of Waterperry, Chelsea and Royal Sovereign are inextricably linked. It is now many years since the last exhibit but many former members of staff and students vividly remember the anxieties, the excitement and, very frequently, the triumphs of those few days in May.

The television programme shown annually by the BBC at the time of each Chelsea Flower Show is headed Growing for Gold, and that is exactly what Beatrix Havergal set out to obtain, the small card left without ceremony at a stand by judges informing all who see it that the stand represents perfection, nothing less. Most gardeners have their favourite plants or crops. Miss H., as stated earlier, was never one for small effects; her main love was fruit with all its problems of production but with results to delight both the eye and the taste buds. In the Royal Sovereign strawberry she had a variety that can still claim to be the finest dessert strawberry ever grown and yet was manageable in the limited space at Waterperry given the necessary skill and dedication.

The first Chelsea Flower Show as such was held in 1913, previous shows having been held in the gardens of the Inner Temple. In the following year, the fateful 1914, there was an exhibit by the Thatcham Fruit and vegetable Farm near Newbury which drew a rather snide comment from the *Gardeners' Magazine*. 'Without being disrespectful to the ladies, we venture to think that mere man is not yet outdone in as far as the art of growing and staging vegetables is concerned.' No doubt the young Beatrix Havergal beginning her training at Thatcham in 1917 was regaled with stories of the Show though she had to wait until 1919 before one was held again. Downe House, Pusey and the beginnings of Waterperry were all absorbing in the years following, and it was not until

1938 that she gained a small foothold as an exhibitor. The first effort consisted of twenty pots of Royal Sovereign plants at the end of someone else's table and all concerned were greatly encouraged by the interest shown by Queen Mary who stopped to admire.

Again Chelsea had to be abandoned, this time for a period of eight years, and it was May 1947 before the Hospital grounds bloomed again. Waterperry repeated its small exhibit and gradually inched its way into the medal reckoning. Space is precious at Chelsea but as confidence grew they applied for more; in 1955 the area available was 35 ft. by 7 ft. 6 in. and the result the first Gold. There are four possible awards for fruit exhibits, rising from a Hogg medal to Silver Hogg, Silver-Gilt Hogg and the coveted Society's Gold. In 1954 the school had been awarded a Hogg medal and a gardening writer covering the Show as a whole wrote 'Waterperry were showing maiden plants of Malling 40 strain of Royal Sovereign, some 15 to 18 inch in diameter. I wouldn't have believed anyone else that they were maidens. Waterperry jolly well deserved their Hogg, not only for excellence but for blazoning forth the fact that certified stock is the only strawberry stock worth growing.' A leap from Hogg to Gold in the following year was a considerable achievement.

'Showing plants' has a certain ring of simplicity; the reality behind any exhibit involves a long hard slog, weeks of coaxing or checking, feeding and adjusting temperatures, watching for pests and problems, all in Waterperry's case to ensure that about three hundred strawberry plants should be able to face a critical public, each bearing perfectly formed and ripe fruit on a certain day. Two factors made the task even more difficult. Whereas the large commercial firms were able to grow plants by the thousand so as to be able to select a few of the best, Waterperry could not spare the space or labour to grow more than they would actually require, and nearly all the plants grown for the purpose were used; there could be little margin for error or accident. Also the strawberry by its very nature is a delicate creature, easily damaged, and Sovereign, as befits a prima donna, more temperamental than most.

The greatest credit for the continued success of the strawberries, bringing Waterperry fifteen Golds in all, must go to Joan Stokes who calmly and methodically brought her beauties up to the post year after year and managed to maintain an optimistic front when all seemed lost. The process started in August when she selected likely plants from the annual layering, potting them up in 6-inch pots which stood out in frames until November. With their growth over for the year they were unceremoniously laid on their sides in a stack against the brick wall of a glasshouse, plant outwards and exposed to all weather but sheltered by the house while straw was packed between the pots. In late January they would be roused from this torpid state and brought into the glasshouses and the three months ritual of feeding, watering, pollinating with a rabbit's foot and just watching began.

Miss H. was of course deeply involved but mainly at consultative and anxiety level, alternating dramatically between hope and despair. She kept a complete record of the plants' progress each year, many of the entries written sitting on the edge of the water tank in No. 2 House and often at midnight when she would combine strawberry watching with the dog's last run. These records remain complete from 1956, the earliest having been stolen at the Show itself together with her camera, and they give a glimpse of the problems involved, many caused by the vagaries of the weather. At the beginning of each year's entry Miss H. would set out the ideal timetable, the stages of development that were hoped for week by week until Chelsea week. Under the ideal came the reality and the 1957 notes give a particularly clear record of events. Houses 1 and 2, now demolished, were good but old-fashioned houses just inside the Kitchen Garden wall, heated by the old coke boilers and requiring real expertise and knowledge for good results.

1957 Forecast:
March 25 Trusses well developed.
April 1 Trusses showing tight flower buds.
April 8 Coming into flower.
April 15 Full flower.
April 22 Thinning.
April 29 Spreading pips and swelling fast.
May 6 Going white, beginning to colour.
May 13 Colouring and ripening.
May 20 Ripe and ready.
Actuality: Warm early season.
March 25: Flower trusses well developed and some coming into flower — thought to be much too far on — but impossible to hold back because of high outside temperatures. At least two weeks ahead. B.H. thinks it impossible to hold them back. Both batches in 1 & 2 have had no heat for weeks but night temperatures too high.
April 1: Both batches coming into flower. Both 1 & 2 most setting, but lot of later trusses which might help. Batch 2 just coming in flower and being pollinated.

April 8: Much colder weather — very cold east wind. May hold them back — houses should be shut to avoid wind but then would be hopeless. Hoping to hold back.
April 15: Both houses look lovely — all spaced out on their staging. Masses of flowers — very little foliage, plants flat looking — have never seen such equality of growth and flowers, such supremacy of flowers over foliage. Cold all last week, some frost at night — lack of foliage perhaps due to cold conditions.
April 22: Batches almost identical — thinning has begun today — back shelf of 1 and 2 furthest on. Largest fruit left — all hard green, to ripen three weeks to a month today. Tables not really ready for thinning.
April 29: No 1 definitely a week behind. In two plants on back shelf most advanced, largest fruits shed petals long ago, now ½ in. x ½ in.
May 3: Last night all strawberries sprayed with Shirlan against mildew, have held back wonderfully, all swelling fast and spreading pips. Thinning completed on the 24th. No 5 contains 102 plants, further in about six fruits pinking. B.H. says are not large enough, J.S. says they are. No 2 week ahead of No 1. Dressing plants everywhere with pinch of Dr Bewby mixture, 5 parts Blood, 1 Potash, 12 Soil. All watered with Solufeed since April 18, also one dressing of blood on first thinning day. Now decided heat at night to keep 60° — foliage risen right above pot, rich green. All depends on weather. Going to keep 1 and 2 closed, only roof air, and use shading to steady temperature.
May 12: One week to go. No. 5 cold house — pots very slow to colour, much better than last year, think most can go to Chelsea. 1 and 2. Both houses much the same, no side air, warm and moist, have come on a great deal. Best plants up on the roof shelves — general impression smaller than last year due to extremely cold conditions at flowering time — but many swelling to good size. All want sorting out again, all best putting on shelves, furthest on north side, most backward on south side. I think we shall be very short of fruit to pick. We want the following, 300 pots to take up, 300 large fruit picked — that's all.
May 20: Magnificently even batch, every plant good. We were given 35 ft. x 7 ft. 6 in., and we took up 317 pots, over 400 picked strawberries. Miracle. Both batches ripened together beautifully and couldn't have been better. The best exhibit we have ever staged. Gold Medal for 3rd time.

Fifteen Gold Medals in sixteen years from 1955 is a fine record and justified all the nervous energy, time and sheer physical effort involved.

The year of the descent to a mere Silver Gilt, 1960, was a particularly difficult one weatherwise, and Miss H.'s notes for the last few days mirror this.

May 16: Our worst ever year, never been in such a quandary, probably ought to have cancelled. Mildew, too hot and dry. Bad pollination certainly due to overcrowding of plants in 1 on tables — carnations far too long in 2. We are not proud of them — afraid not able to make a decent exhibit. I know that I have deserted the strawberries more than usual, owing to inexperienced staff on so much of the place.
May 23rd: Fruit overripe, poor shape and colour. However the Queen and Sir David Bowes-Lyon came to see them, we produced dish for the Queen. Exhibit a miracle, but not good quality, so Silver Gilt.

But even most of the Gold-winning years had their bad moments, and the notes read rather like the temperature chart of a high fever. In 1959 for instance we read:

May 15th: I am really concerned now, poorly developed fruit, badly pollinated. I fear mildew — Joan S. does not agree, thinks they are ripening normally.
Three days later:
May 18th: A lovely sight! Result, the fifth Gold. In 1962 the strawberries were 'all behind — laggards!' Everything hung on the weather, but all came right in the last two weeks to give the seventh Gold, the 'loveliest ever'.

In 1963 the fruit was very unripe but Princess Margaret seems to have saved the day by remarking how attractive the green berries looked and how nice it was to have some to follow on. 1965 brought problems of staging for some reason, and Miss H. notes that it was a masterpiece of good management by Joan Stokes who should have an award herself. The Garden Club of America had been in raptures. 1966 seems to have been trouble free, so much so that the Duke of Edinburgh suggested that they had all been 'bought in' for the exhibit. 1967 by contrast was a troubled year 'Cloud over exhibit. I know we ought to have cancelled but know we cannot afford NOT to be at Chelsea. Need cash from sale of plants — if we're not there thought to be suffering from the same treatment as Studley. Hoping for support . . . can count on young staff.' But it was Gold number 12, and Miss H. noted that in the following year she must visit the glasshouse to check midnight temperatures. She certainly followed this up as in May 1968 we find an ecstatic entry. 'I feel like purring as a cat as I look at them, sitting on the water tank summing them up. If this is to be the last time we shall have triumphed with the best we have ever produced. A labour of love from all hard-working staff.' It was the thirteenth Gold. The fourteenth was achieved in spite of 'problems all the way' and a great many night walks with Bruce, the current dog. Gold 15 was the one bright spot of 1970, darkened by Miss S.'s increasing ill-health and her death in August.

In the more difficult years one wonders if some of the students — or even one or two members of staff — wondered whether the game was worth the candle, worth the tension, the strained atmosphere in the house when all was not going to plan, the channelling of energies at a time when Second Years were thinking of final examinations and futures. Undoubtedly Chelsea did help to keep Waterperry in the public eye and in the forefront regarding plant sales. Anything from 25,000 strawberry plants and upwards were produced annually in the West Field, and the cash was desperately needed. But probably the greatest value lay in the satisfaction of playing some part in staging perfection, of reaching, just for two or three days, the highest possible standard.

The problems of getting the fruiting plants ready at exactly the right time were at least spread over months; the last and most taxing operations involved packing, transporting and staging. A lettuce crate was prepared for each pair of pots, empty pots being used first to make the moulds in quantities of wood wool and cotton wadding, finished with tissue paper, shiny side up. Great care was taken to leave a groove round each pot so that the fruit could hang clear, and the rims of the travelling pots were padded. Each plant had been carefully thinned and would have about eight or nine of the largest and choicest fruit — before they travelled Joan Stokes wrapped each individual berry in a six inch square of tissue paper. Nothing was left to chance. The precious plants were installed in their crates and were driven up to Chelsea on the Friday leaving Saturday and Sunday for the staging process.

Weeks before the Day the students had collected tiny hazel twigs, cut them to size and painted them green to make crutches for the fruit, and in this way the stems were supported above soil level. Some leaves also had to be pinned down or across the pot so as to help the artistic impression and to help conceal the pot which was swathed in green cotton material. The Show organizers only supplied a large trestle table, backing on to the outside wall of the marquee and never in the same place two years running. Despite annual appeals from her staff Miss H. refused to have a permanent framework made, declaring that the whole procedure would become too easy and predictable, leaving no room for inspiration. That may have been so, but the elaborate arrangement of boxes, adjusted and propped to provide a base for the required pyramids was difficult to achieve and time consuming. Proceedings were not hastened by Miss H.'s delight in long conversations with other Chelsea habituees when they passed the stand. Joan Stokes and Jean Manger with second year students were the most regular helpers and a great deal depended on whether that particular 'intake' had any feeling for display work. Every box was covered with black velvet where it showed and black cotton where it did not, purely for economy — shades of Sheridan's *Critic* with Tilburina and her Confidant, and no doubt the stagers felt stretched to the limits of sanity at times. But the final result was always magical, bright berries, suspended with little obvious support, arranged in two or three pyramids varying according to the amount of fruit available. Two notice-boards in green and white spelling out Waterperry's title and address completed the exhibition with some green foliage, perhaps pots of grevillea, to soften the ends of the staging. All was nearly complete for the Private Day and Henry Guy was left to guard the fruit over Sunday night, the chief marauders being on-duty policemen and a blackbird of great perspicacity who took up residence in the top of the great marquee year after year with one object in view.

Monday is the 'Royals' Day and the only strawberry fit for a Queen had to be provided. Very early in the morning Joan Stokes picked ripe fruit from the pots remaining at Waterperry, delivering them to the Show in wooden trays lined again with wadding and tissue paper. These were arranged in patterns on large oval green plates, and the plates propped to show to full advantage in the spaces in front of the pyramids, completing the picture. Everything is done on the Monday at Chelsea to ensure that the Royal Family have a private visit, and only two people were allowed to man each exhibit. Miss H. in best suit and what has been described as an 'almost frilly hat' together with Miss S. more elegantly dressed, remained, although only one was really visible. Even in those surroundings Miss S. managed to merge into the backcloth. The other workers contrived on occasions to hover in the Ladies Room long enough to evade discovery by the officials and then concealed themselves behind the staging to catch a glimpse of the Queen; if thwarted they could often console themselves with a close-up of rehearsals for Trooping the Colour at the Chelsea barracks.

The prospect of meeting the Queen and offering a sample Royal Sovereign — invariably accepted — added to the excitement and joy of the occasion. There was always the absorbing question as to what the Royals would do with their stalks. Prince Philip usually strode to the staging and flicked the stalk underneath, the Queen's was rumoured to pass from hand to hand, lady-in-waiting to equerry and so on until it was lost. For several years when there was sufficient fruit Miss H. personally delivered a basket of strawberries to the Palace and received a gracious acknowledgement. Fruit was even sent up in 1971, the last year of the School when no exhibit was possible, and the Queen sent a message through Sir John Miller that she was sad to learn that Waterperry was giving up and she hoped the Royal Sovereign might be saved. A few years later Her Majesty's gardener from Windsor came to collect an order of plants from Waterperry to replace an old bed in the Royal gardens so one hopes the Queen is still enjoying that uniquely flavoured fruit. In April of 1971 the President of the Royal Horticultural Society, Lord Aberconway, wrote to Miss H. 'I was sad indeed to hear that you won't be able to show your strawberries at Chelsea this year. The Show will not be the same without you and certainly not so good . . . wise to yield to the inevitable, sad tho' it is.'

Of course not all Chelsea week was deadly serious and we can catch a glimpse of this in an amusing letter written by Hilda Murrell to Cynthia Havergal, Miss H.'s cousin and Hilda Murrell's great friend in 1974, some years before Miss Murrell's tragic and still unsolved murder. Miss H. and Havergal Two, as she was affectionately known at Waterperry, visited Chelsea after Miss H.'s retirement and Cynthia wrote of this visit to her friend, the daughter of Edwin Murrell, rose-grower in her own right. Hilda Murrell wrote: 'It must have been a real tonic to get on to the old stamping ground again. I never was in the glory of the President's marquee. Honestly however I can't think how Chelsea survives without our two exhibits, they were both unique in their kinds, though hers of course much more glorious than mine. Nor can I think how the Queen gets through that dreary evening with no horses and not even any strawberries . . . Usually they were opposite me, and the royal couple stood and guzzled Waterperry's best, throwing the stalks over their shoulders on to my miniature roses. But there was one year when they were right down at the other end of the big marquee. HM arrived at the magic spot. "Where are the strawberries?" she says, loud and clear. So they set off at a smart pace, ignoring all other exhibits including of course poor little me. A few minutes later enter B.H. I said, "The Queen's on her way to your stand." She said, 'Where are the strawberries?'" Exit B.H. at a run.'

The Royal Sovereign strawberry is already losing ground at Waterperry and inferior varieties are superseding the Chelsea favourite. This is not entirely philistinism — financial pressures are considerable in horticulture as in other businesses and it is tempting to go for a tougher more prolific crop even if the fruit tastes of nothing in particular. The increasing popularity of Pick-your-own establishments show that the general public enjoys a day in the open air but cares little for real quality, yet it would be sad if the Royal Sovereign was discarded completely. If that happens visitors must take heart from the one permanent record remaining. If they go into the church they will find the plants in the beautiful Waterperry window designed by King of Norwich in 1971, a record in stained glass of a real effort to produce perfection.

Chapter Thirteen

The gardens at Waterperry have been open to the public for at least a decade, yet even now people who live locally are often unaware of their extensiveness and charm. Visitors who hesitate at the entrance looking across the former Kitchen Garden can see no further than the mellow brick walls, reputedly built by French prisoners in the Napoleonic Wars. The superb old copper beech, beckoning above the wall, should give them heart to explore further.

Mrs O'Connor's enchantingly overgrown Kitchen Garden was soon brought to order as essential to the programme of training, but the purely ornamental garden beyond the wall had to wait considerably longer. Miss H., while longing to beautify and expand the grounds, always put the educational needs first. The students, in a relatively short time, had to master many techniques in as broad a curriculum as possible while, at the same time, producing saleable crops for income. So Miss H.'s ideas — and she was full of them — could only be developed in fits and starts when there was a little time or perhaps when some crop had brought in a profit. She was prepared to take infinite pains over details of any horticultural innovation, and one of her great gifts as a gardener was her instinctive knowledge of what to plant, where to plant and when, something that can not really be found in books on the subject.

In 1934 almost immediately after her arrival at Waterperry she was encouraged by gifts of plants from another well-known woman gardener, the eccentric and rather tragic Miss Ellen Willmott. Ellen Willmott inherited Warley Place in Middlesex from her parents while still a young woman, and lavished her considerable wealth on creating a superb garden there, together with several other gardens abroad. It was said that at one period she employed no fewer than eighty gardeners at Warley alone. However, even if it seems unlikely that she did much in the way of practical gardening herself, she was a very knowledgeable plantswoman and collector. She was also very musical, and met the young Beatrix Havergal when they were both singing in the London Bach Choir.

Impoverished and embittered at the end of her life and forced to abandon Warley she gave a number of treasured plants from the Warley garden to her young friend for Waterperry. The one still most evident is the Ailanthus Wilsonae, the 'Tree of Heaven' which survived removal from Middlesex to Oxfordshire as quite a big tree and which can be seen on the large lawn behind the shrub borders. Another of her gifts, contrasting in size, can be found in the front of the shrub border, the creamy white iris-like spikes of Sisyrinchium striatum, the Satin flower from China.

Digging for Victory absorbed any extra energies during the war years. In 1951 the Horticultural School was featured in an article in the *Women and Beauty* magazine, written in a truly glossy style by Jean Cleland. Her meeting with Miss H. in the house sets the tone. 'A large square hall, cool with stone flags, and bright with tall vases of flowers. Stags' heads hung on the walls, an old gate-legged table, polished to the sheen of watered silk stood in the middle of the room and, except for the slow ticking of a grandfather clock, it was so quiet that I almost jumped when Miss Havergal, the Principal of the School, came in.' Miss H.'s measured tread must have been unusually muffled that day, but the writer goes on to describe her appearance both accurately and charmingly, as 'dressed in green smock, gardening breeches and knitted stockings, all of which, with her tall figure and short grey hair, infinitely became her.'

The reporter was then taken out to be introduced to the students and to see the gardens. The most photogenic of the set, a slim fair girl called Judy Fletcher, was marked out for star treatment, and a series of photographs taken showing her engaged in various gardening activities, being instructed by Rosemary Dobereiner in the use of a wheel hoe, watering plants on the conservatory staging and so on. The collection of photographs was very attractive but rather too clean and tidy to be realistic, the young star depicted without a hair out of place, immaculate in white shirt and green dungarees. It would have been interesting to know if any young readers of the magazine were inspired to become lady gardeners as a result of reading the article.

1952 saw an attempt to create a formal Rock Garden following on from the herbaceous border and towards the river. This had been a dream for some time, but an early attempt on the further side of the bridge was abandoned. A large pine tree occupied the site, and this was cut down for a start to be made. Miss H. was a cine-camera enthusiast and filmed the whole operation; the film was shown to successive years of students, first forward and then backwards, always accompanied by hoots of mirth from Miss H. as the tree returned to its place. A start was made on the project, first year students moving vast quantities of soil under the guidance of Pam Schwerdt, and a small Alpine area was planted and cared for by Valerie Finnis. Eventually the area as we now know it was completed by an outside firm, much to Miss H.'s disappointment. Writing to Douglas Chalk of Gavin Jones Nurseries Limited she explained, 'I take particular interest in the placing of the rocks, and would give anything to have the time to do this myself, because I want the finished result to look as natural as possible.' There was a considerable amount of heavy work involved, and Mr Chalk's estimate makes that clear. It runs 'Supply all necessary tackle and labour for the moving of your existing rocks to the required site. Dig out rocks from the area below the stone bridge and construct to form natural outcrops on the bank above the bridge. Excavate soil as necessary to build up and undulate the ground. Tie rock work into existing stones now supporting the bridge and adjust certain of existing formations to conform with the new design. Clean up and leave tidy.'

Douglas Chalk visited Waterperry in October when he discussed the project with Valerie Finnis and then wrote to Miss H. saying that he thought the bank was ideally suited and sufficient stone — from the earlier attempt — was available; it was just possible that he might need to import one really large piece for a 'bold feature'. A sketch of the suggested layout followed which Miss H. acknowledged three months later, conceding that the design was most attractive. The stones were once again her main interest. 'I should like to see the stones tilting more backwards into the ground,' she wrote, 'following the natural strata of this particular local limestone.' The work was completed in February, 1961, by three men from the nursery, the total cost being under one hundred pounds. The men could not be accommodated in the house, but were put up at the Station Hotel in Wheatley at a cost of 15/- per night for bed and breakfast, and could get a three-course lunch at the Bungalow Café for 3/9. The Rock Garden is now part of the accepted landscape, seemingly 'as natural as possible' and a very attractive feature of the garden.

In 1962 all attention was focused on the opposite side of the house and Miss Kitson's Lecture Block, but at the end of 1963 plans were afoot to remove a rather poor rose bed in the South Field, beside the cordon apples, and replace it with an Island Bed. Island Beds, beds of irregular shape that could be walked round and so seen from all angles, were being developed at this time by Alan Bloom, of Bressingham fame. They were a conscious effort to revive interest in herbaceous plants which were losing favour with the general public while breaking away from the formal border, beautiful but time-consuming and requiring a background to show it off to its best effect. It was to Alan Bloom that Waterperry turned for advice concerning this new bed. The result is now part of the scenery and so matured that it is hard to visualize the area without it. But it is interesting to discover just how much correspondence and planning was needed to make a successful bed. Amateurs are prone to think — or hope — that garden beds just happen, while the professional knows all too well that it must be made to happen. Miss H., we know, had the capacity to make things happen, but little time, hence the approach to Alan Bloom who seems to have been delighted at the idea.

Once again Valerie Finnis made the first contact and it was to her that Alan Bloom wrote just before Christmas, 1963. 'Now, about this Island Bed. I'm fairly certain I remember the site and it should be a pretty good one. And it does me good (or at least my ego) not only to think of Perennials taking the place of roses, but because Mr Hudson suggested it when he called at Waterperry — suggested an Island Bed, I mean. I'd like to help but must warn you that it isn't easy to follow a prepared plan when it comes to planting beds of irregular shape. Still, this need not deter you but what I would find difficult, unless fully informed of your stocks, would be knowing what to include of those you do not have. Could you let me use my discretion about using substitutes from here where I considered any of yours to be unsuitable or superseded? Your suggestion of an intersecting path is a good one but I would say it would be better if the corners were rather more rounded like this.' Here he included a sketch of the proposed beds. 'Do you agree? And how wide would you like to have the path, taking account of wear and tear assuming it will be grass? As a rough estimate the bed will hold about a thousand plants if a good effect is wanted in the first year. I'm asking all this now because I'd rather make the plan during the present slack time.'

Miss H. now took up the correspondence with Alan Bloom. 'It is extraordinarily kind of you to help in the planning of this bed. For a long time we have disliked the roses that have merely existed in this bed for some reason unknown to us, and there is no doubt that it would be an enormous improvement to the herbaceous nursery to have a good show of herbaceous plants in that particular bed. Therefore we are clearing the roses, deeply digging and manuring, and it would be a great excitement to have your help with regard to the choice of plant and arrangement. We have made a rough plan of the bed, measured in 3 feet squares, and I think it can be relied upon to give you the approximate shape and size of the area. I love your idea of splitting the bed with that attractive and natural looking path, and think it is an excellent plan. You will, I am sure, arrange for a suitable width of that path, but my opinion would be that it should be at least 3 feet wide at one end and perhaps narrowing to 2 feet at the other. I am sending our list of herbaceous plants only for reference, and would like to make it perfectly clear that it is to be a "show bed" of real interest to visitors. At the same time we do need to consider people ordering plants from what they have seen, and we would like to be able to supply them from our own nursery — so if a proportion could be from the Waterperry list we could save the cost of planting.'

Alan Bloom in his reply promised to send a list of the best plants for the bed so that Waterperry could mark off what they had available; he would supply the rest. He then discussed the planning and planting. 'I could send you the plan in advance of the plants from here so that planting may commence, as placing and spacing the groups is apt to be somewhat tricky at first. I gather you would like me to do the actual planning, but do assure you that it is not difficult to map out on the spot if labels on sticks are used to plot out the group positions. It is sadly true that a great deal of juggling is usually necessary when following a prepared plan of an irregularly shaped bed in order to fit everything in correctly. I usually begin in the centre and work outwards. I would suggest varying the size of groups according to the growth of the plant, but would you prefer the easier method of having uniform group spaces, and varying the quantity to suit?'

Miss H. wrote back by return strongly vetoing the 'easier method'. 'Please do vary the size of groups — I should hate uniform grouped spaces and we will most certainly do our best to reproduce your design. I cannot imagine anything worse than planting everything in the same sized spaces. I once saw a long herbaceous border in a College garden where everything was planted in squares at the back of the border and two parallel lines of dwarf plants running the full length of the border in the front. It will give us enormous pleasure to have the fun of reproducing whatever you draw on the plan, and we will do any necessary juggling. It will be a great excitement to have this adventure. I feel quite certain it is going to be a show border which will be of great interest to us all and our many visitors, and we will publish the fact that it has been planned by you if you would like us to do so.'

Alan Bloom returned the plan speedily so that the area could be marked out and labelled before the Bressingham plants arrived, and added a few more hints for ease of planting. 'The quantities of each kind vary a little according to spread; though a good deal of juggling may be necessary before spacing is ready, the way to do this is to use tags on canes as markers, each tag carrying the group number. There are 58 groups in the section on the left of the path, and 62 on the right. It is important in all cases to allow a good 25% more of space between each group than between individual plants comprising each group.'

The scene was now set for action though, as so often happens in gardening, the weather nearly had the last word. As soon as the Bressingham plants had been dispatched there was continuous heavy rain and planting was impossible. On arrival every plant had to be unwrapped and plunged into peat beds in open frames, involving double handling, and considerable frustration for all involved. But eventually the bed was planted and has flourished, with most of the original plants intact. One hoped-for benefit regarding Island Beds did not materialize; Alan Bloom had expected that the plants, receiving light from all sides as opposed to those backed by a wall or hedge, would not require staking, a time-consuming task. The Waterperry beds were not staked in their first season with the result that taller plants fell flat and threatened to smother others. It is now staked by the method of laying twiggy branches over the plants in the early stages to that they grow up through the branches and remain erect.

Miss H.'s final addition was probably most dear to her heart, the planting of the long rose border at the river end of the garden. She loved roses and had made several attempts over the years to grow them in spite of Mrs O'Connor's gloomy prediction that they would not do well. Her earliest attempt to have rose beds in front of the house had been thwarted by Magdalen College's warning as to the 'liabilities of pleasure-gardens'. In her last years she was to make one more effort. The long border, previously devoted to plum trees, was cleared, cultivated deeply and manured, and for one season grew up a magnificent crop of runner beans. During that time, in 1967, Jean Manger and Mary Spiller visited the famous family firm of rose growers, John Mattocks, who were usually to be among the Chelsea Gold medal winners. There they selected varieties for the new border and it was duly planted up in 1968. While not an unqualified success the border was a great improvement on previous efforts. Miss H. at last had her roses, and the silver rose bowl presented to her by former students on her retirement was a fitting gift.

After Miss H.'s death it was decided to refurbish the rose border in her memory. Previously it had been backed by a lonicera hedge on the north side, effectively screening the roses from the rest of the ornamental garden and placing it in the South Field. This hedge was grubbed out and a yew hedge planted on the south side, a semicircular area paved for seats in the centre, and a low edging of lavender planted in the front. In summer it was a peaceful scented spot, valued by visitors in need of a rest, and from the seats they caught glimpses of the house and the church, both so dear to Miss H.'s heart.

Chapter Fourteen

By 1962 women gardeners would seem to have come a long way from the 'ladies in bloomers at Kew'. But there was still considerable prejudice against women, not so much in the private sector as in that relating to work with public authorities. Miss H. was always a doughty fighter for her girls' opportunities, and back in 1952 we find her sounding out various Parks Superintendents for their views on employing women, by means of a duplicated letter. 'Dear Sir, I have a student who is leaving me at the end of July after two years' training in general horticulture, and she is anxious to get into Public Parks work. She is 22 and had two years practical experience before coming here, four years experience in all. I am not sure what the opportunities are for women in this branch of horticulture, and should be most grateful if you would let me know whether you think there is scope for her. She is very keen to do it, and would, I think, be a useful person particularly in the propagation department.'

It is not certain whether this student actually existed or whether Miss H. was just 'flying the kite' but her letter certainly brought a crop of surprisingly cold and discouraging replies. Only Coventry gave any encouragement; they would be advertising in the *Gardeners' Chronicle* in the near future specifically for a woman gardener, and the Waterperry student's application would be considered. Other replies ranged from the indifferent to the hostile. The Parks Superintendent of Northampton addressed his letter 'Dear Sir' hardly a tactful start, and continued, 'In reply to your letter of the 5th July we do NOT employ girls on horticultural work in this department. The large City Parks Departments may perhaps employ a few in the greenhouses, but I would say that vacancies for women in public park work are very restricted.'

Leamington Spa was hedging his bets. 'Whilst of the considered opinion that there is ample scope for people of this type in Public Parks Departments I regret, owing to the general working accommodation and conditions that I am not in a position to offer this young lady a suitable post. It may be to her advantage to apply to some of the larger departments.' Nottingham obviously considered women as merely casual labour. 'The only occasion on which we engage female gardeners is for part-time work during studies or during vacations: there is very little outlet for them in municipal parks.' Derby reluctantly admitted to having one or two Lady Gardeners who had lingered on from the war years, but gave his personal opinion that chances to get on beyond ordinary gardening work were very remote. He did, however, admit that Lady Gardeners could excel in many sections of horticulture. Birmingham had no vacancies, while Cheltenham was 'extremely doubtful whether opportunities would ever arise to allow women to advance in public park horticulture.'

This discouraging response seems extraordinary today, and how delighted Miss H. would have been to know that a woman is currently in charge of the Royal Parks in London. But this must have been the final trumpeting before lowering the flag of male domination, since it was not long before Waterperry girls did manage to find posts in Public Parks. Even then there was a battle to be won for full recognition of the standard of the Waterperry training itself. A letter, dated 29th January 1959, to J. R. B. Evison, Superintendent of the Brighton Parks and Gardens Department explains the problems.

> I have one student working in Ealing Parks who has been there for two or three years and seems to be doing very good work in the glasshouses. She now writes to me in considerable concern as she finds that, with the new arrangements with regard to the pay and grading scheme she is now classified as 'Gardener uncertified; Class 1'; from this she gathers that her Waterperry Diploma has not been recognized and it seems that she is now downgraded.
>
> She is working for the new examination for a Certificated Gardener and has sent me a copy of the syllabus which seems similar to the syllabus for our Diploma with the exception of the Parks aspect of laying out ornamental grounds, recreation areas, etc. I presume if she passes this examination successfully she will then be upgraded again. From what she tells me the only Diplomas that are recognized are those from Wisley and Kew, and both these places have only men students. It seems that a number of women are being taken into Parks work, and I was interested to hear that the London Parks are wanting women and are hoping that some of our girls would consider working there. If women are able to do good work and are acceptable for Park

work it would seem that they should have the same chance of advancement as men.

As our people seem to be wanted, is it possible that our Diploma can be recognized as a qualification? I do not feel happy that these good girls should be considered 'Uncertificated Gardeners'. The one at Ealing got a 'First' in the R.H.S. General and a First Class Diploma from here, and I cannot agree that she is an Uncertificated Gardener. I realize the Waterperry Diploma cannot carry weight until our training is better known, but I would like to tell you that last July we had a full three day inspection by the Ministry of Education and Agriculture. We had applied to the Ministry for recognition under Rule 16 as an efficient training place, and we have now received that recognition and a very encouraging and excellent report. I shall be most grateful for any advice you can give me.

The qualification for Certificated Gardeners, needed by Parks employees and laid down by the National Joint Council for Local Authorities Services (Manual Workers) was five years practical experience or apprenticeship and a pass in a practical and written examination or Diploma from Edinburgh, or the Internal Examination of the Institute of Park Administration. Mr Evison in his reply appreciated Miss H.'s anxiety and was firmly on her side. 'If your girl at Ealing is carrying out the duties of a Certificated Gardener as set out in the definitions then I should think she had been hardly dealt with and could make an appeal for reconsideration without there being any question of the Waterperry Diploma being considered at all. The Examination for Certificated Gardener, as I understand it, would be a simple affair and one that anyone who has your Diploma would not need to study for.' The question of a list of examinations that would qualify for exemption was a more difficult problem. Mr Evison suggested that there were many excellent horticultural examinations which might be more than adequate, and he quoted Writtle as one example. But equally he knew of some undesirables which it would be difficult to exclude once the door was opened. Hence the very short list of three, of which only Edinburgh was then open to women. He thought Miss H. had a valid point and, since the Institute had no intention of discriminating against women, he thought they might like an opportunity to reconsider.

Miss H., encouraged, stated her case in a letter to L. E. Morgan, the Hon-General Secretary to the Institute of Park Administration and received the following reply in May of 1960, 'In as far as the Waterperry

Diploma is concerned the Committee (Training and Examinations of the Local Government Examination Board) was pleased to accept my recommendation that it should be placed on the same basis as the Wisley — Kew — Edinburgh Diplomas, as being one of the places open to girl students and allowed for exemption purposes. For some years I have been concerned that girls should have equal opportunities for employment in the public parks service as young men; this is now accepted in its entirety.'

One more small hurdle remained, the recognition of the Waterperry Diploma as the appropriate qualification for women applying for Associate Membership of the Institute of Park Administration and this recognition was granted in May, 1962. Waterperry was at last recognized as ranking with the best training places in the country.

It should be pointed out that this final accolade would not have been thought of by either Principal as a victory for women's rights, or part of any such movement. They just wanted their system of training acknowledged to be as good as anything obtained in the men's establishment, and that the holders of the Waterperry Diploma, who happened to be women, were known to be perfectly capable of holding important posts in Public Departments. Miss H.'s determination to gain parity in these aspects even led her to query a ruling on the tools supplied to candidates taking practical tests and to take a line that must have been rather unexpected. Writing to Dr Taylor, the then Chairman of the Examination Board she complained that women candidates were being provided with smaller spades and forks. 'I feel sure most of them would prefer to use the standard tools as provided for all candidates and would not want to be singled out for preferential treatment. I would feel that there would be a danger of inferior and inadequate tools being provided, and many would object to having to use them.'

This stance seems to be trying to equate parity of esteem with equality of muscle power, and, while Miss H. had plenty of the latter and weight to back it, I suspect that some of her smaller students were only too pleased to be offered lighter equipment. Fortunately for them the Examination Board were ready to compromise; two sets of tools would be supplied in future and candidates would be able to choose.

Another subject that exercised Miss H., as it does all employers, was that of wages. Her attitude, where her students were concerned, was of a piece with the Waterperry ethos, and a letter to a would-be employer of a former student in 1958 makes this clear. 'With regard to salary, I always recommend students to begin at a low figure to enable them to prove their worth, which I always hope will be recognized after the first six months, so that they can look forward to the incentive of a rise if they are satisfactory. Jackie will be 21 in November and therefore will be entitled to the full minimum agricultural wage which is £5-14-0 per week, and my recommendation to my students is for them to ask £1 per week more than the minimum in view of the two years' training that they have had. This makes £6-14-0, from which can be deducted the agriculture allowance for board, i.e. £2-4-0 which means that they then receive £4-10-0 per week clear of living. I have often suggested to them that they should ask £4 per week clear of living, hoping for an increase of 10/- per week after the first six months if satisfactory.'

In the same year Miss H. was giving advice to an older student who had trained from 1949 to 51. She had been employed by the Cambridge Botanic Gardens in the September of 1956 as a student gardener at the princely wage of £6 per week. In the following February she had been given entire responsibility for the Alpine Department, yet still remained at £6 on the pretext that a position for staff, as opposed to student, had not been established in the Rock Garden and had to be confirmed by the Professor; she was not recognized as Staff until August when her wages rose to £8. Early in the following year all staff had a 7/6d increase, so she earned £8-7-6, but for this had the entire responsibility of both Rock Gardens, the Alpine House and all that entailed, while having to train a student under her. She knew, as only a Waterperry girl could know, that she was working far harder and with more interest than most of the staff; she also knew that folk with no skill or knowledge were earning more, and she would be grateful for Miss H.'s opinion. 'My knowledge of alpine plants is all that there is in the garden,' she wrote, 'there is none to advise me and I do just what I think.'

Miss H. answered fairly quickly though with the usual apology — 'It is difficult to sit in in the daytime.' Her answer highlights the problems still facing women, and the different attitude taken to the theoretical gardener as opposed to the practical. 'I think the question of wage is going to be a difficult problem always on the purely practical side of gardening and it is a frequent bone of contention that those doing educational work get a higher rate of pay than the practical gardener does. Administration and advisory work and teaching will always command a higher wage, provided the person is qualified with the B.Sc. or NDH. I entirely agree that you should be getting more than £8-7-6 particularly if you have sole charge of the whole rock gardens. I do not know how Cambridge Botanic Gardens had the face only to give you £6 from September '56 to Feb. '57;

It was a wicked wage for someone of your age, experience and education. But these Botanic Gardens are inclined to think that it is a privilege to work in them and that counts as part payment. You should be getting £9 or more in view of the responsibility of your job, and they could not get a man with your knowledge for the money they are giving you. I strongly advise you to try and get an improvement; state your case carefully. I don't want to suggest that you should leave, but I do think your employer should know that you are not content. If they can't pay more they can't, but I cannot believe it. Your knowledge would be so valuable to a nurseryman; there is a younger girl now at Hilliers and in charge of their Alpine exhibit at Chelsea, highly delighted with herself and earning £9 per week.'

The level of wages, even allowing for the vast changes over the last thirty years, seems incredibly low and young apprentices of today who take home about £80 per week before they have acquired skills and without obligation to be willing, helpful or friendly can count themselves rich in material terms. It goes without saying that Miss H. was not so keen on a sound wages structure when she was the employer. In 1964 a former student was offered the post of Assistant Staff in the Glass Department at £5-5-0 clear of living costs, out of which she would have to pay 9/8 National Insurance. It does not seem over-generous, but could be said to be par for the course and, as in the Botanic Gardens, it was a privilege to work at Waterperry. Miss H. certainly had not the resources to pay more, but she hated parting with any money even to her loyal staff, and it was quite an embarrassment to have to ask for wages when on occasions, they failed to materialize at the correct time.

Chapter Fifteen

The celebrations for the award of the Victorian Medal of Honour in 1966 marked the last high point for the Waterperry School. The medal, the highest award the Royal Horticultural Society can make, was instituted in 1897, the year of Queen Victoria's Jubilee, and the list of holders is limited to sixty-three, the years of Victoria's reign. In 1966 Beatrix Havergal was only the eighth woman, including the Queen Mother, to gain this highly prized award; indeed, from its inception in 1897 when two of the first holders were women, no other woman had received it until 1942. All Waterperry basked in reflected glory and after the Award had been published the morning work-reading had a festive air. Large letters reading Congratulations, Miss V.M.H. were held up for Miss H. to read, much to her embarrassment and surprise. A letter of congratulation from P.M. Synge, Secretary of the RHS, gave her much pleasure. 'There is no place I would sooner send a girl who wanted to know how to grow plants than Waterperry.' Members of staff went up to London to see the award-giving ceremony on 23rd February, and everyone celebrated at Waterperry on 25th February. The students presented Miss H. with an eighteen 'carat' necklace, comprising eighteen carrots on a piece of string and, more enduringly, a garden seat; Miss S.'s part was recognized with the gift of a brooch.

Miss H.'s birthday present from the students in July of the same year was a croquet set, a present which, incidentally, was never used. Garden seats and croquet speak eloquently of retirement and leisure, and perhaps the students, unwittingly, were telling both Principals to look to the future. In many respects the writing was already on the wall. Financially the school's affairs were in poor shape. The tremendous price rises in all commodities and equipment without corresponding rises in the price of produce could only be countered by a full complement of students, and this never materialized. Nineteen were in residence in the year of the VMH, the following years saw only fourteen on the roll. The last year to complete the training, entering in September 1969, were good as regards quality but only numbered ten. By then revival was out of the question.

The Royal Sovereign strawberries continued to reign supreme at Chelsea with Gold Medals in 1967 to 1970 inclusive, perhaps masking the fact to the outside world that all was not well. Both Principals were showing signs of strain, Miss S. physically and Miss H. mentally. Her lectures were becoming repetitive, and she was having difficulty in getting through the syllabus, hence the Cucumber Riot of 1967. The same group grumbled that fruit lectures seldom got beyond the 'in phrase', "Dig a hole, girls," and it would have been wiser to have handed these over to the Head of the Fruit Department. Amazingly she still found the energy to drive long distances and lecture to Horticultural Societies, her favourite subjects being Waterperry from its beginnings, Strawberry Growing, and the Herbaceous Border. She had always been a lively, enthusiastic and much sought after speaker, and she enjoyed showing her own films on these subjects. Now the vital spark was dimming and the whole future of Waterperry in jeopardy. Her staff, some of whom had been with her all their working lives, lacked the courage to tackle her on the subject and were inhibited by feelings of affection and loyalty. It was a second year student who had the courage — or the effrontery — to suggest to Miss H. that her school was deteriorating and that both Principals should retire. The staff were horrified, but her action may have initiated an eleventh hour attempt at change.

To do Miss H. justice, in spite of her apparent tardiness in securing a future for the school, she had been aware of this problem for some time. She had always hoped that Waterperry might become a County Training Centre but, characteristically, was only willing for Oxfordshire to have it on her terms, with herself very much in charge. A certain incompatibility with another strong-minded woman, the then County Horticultural Adviser, made Miss H. more determined to hold on to the reins as long as possible; by the time her overall competence could be questioned the county was no longer interested.

In 1969 Miss H. drew up a detailed memorandum 'Notes on the possible future role in the education service for Adults of Waterperry School of Horticulture, prepared and presented by the Principal.' The paper listed Waterperry's assets, gave a résumé of its past history and the ongoing work with students and amateurs and, finally, its aspirations for the future. Miss H. here envisaged Waterperry as a centre providing Diploma courses as before, while adding short courses, resident or otherwise, for teachers and demonstrators, and interested adults. Copies of this document were sent to most influential horticulturists in the country, Heads of Research Stations such as Long Ashton and East Malling, Heads of Botanic Gardens and Parks, University Professors, local worthies and stars of the 'media' like Percy Thrower and Roy Hay, asking for advice and suggestions. One institution approached was the National Trust, Miss H. suggesting that she could extend the Diploma Course to three years with special reference to the training of girls for posts in the Trust Gardens. The National Trust Secretary at that time, whose daughter had trained at Waterperry, was naturally sympathetic. However the Trust was just rethinking its own policies towards its gardens. It had had to abandon its own apprenticeship scheme, the problem being that, since the Trust could not afford salary scales equivalent to those in Parks Department, trainees were only too often lost to them after training. On the other hand Parks staff worked on modern layouts, changing with fashion, while the Trust policy was to adhere to the concept of the original owner. Heads of Park Departments were not likely therefore to move over to National Trust work. Whatever the results of the Trust's rethinking Miss H.'s approach fell on rather stony ground and was never seriously discussed.

Advice came in in plenty, some very good, some, of the 'Waterperry must be kept going at all costs' variety, merely wishful thinking. Often there was a heartfelt lament for standards about to be lost. A member of the East Malling staff wrote in despair, 'Waterperry. It's crystal clear. Here is an excellent training establishment of real quality and of high reputation. The fact is, it merits continuance and development. There is hardly anywhere today that does real plantsmanship. All are for large scale productivity, machines and more machines. Proper use of hand-tools is no longer taught properly anywhere. Frankly I cannot see any support coming from our "masters" for the quality individual. So, if people of high standards fade away there will be no support.'

A friend of Miss H.'s, well known in Oxfordshire educational circles, pin-pointed the problems faced by small private enterprises and, probably without realizing it, echoed the ideas set out in the first prospectus. 'To attract girls who have been in country boarding-schools — often restlessly in their last years — cannot be easy. Their one ambition seems so often to be to live independently in London in a flat, and the thought of more years in a residential country community does not readily appeal. I would think that it was very important, both from the point of view of recruitment and for keeping the students happy when they come, to make the most of the opportunities Oxford has to offer. I am not thinking solely of opportunities of meeting young men socially, although this is a necessary part of it, but also of enabling them to have a real share in music, acting, and all the other activities. I have wondered in this connection too, whether any link-up would be possible with the Lady Spencer-Churchill Training College, so near to you?'

The most perspicacious comment came from the then RHS Secretary. 'The commonest observation I have heard about Waterperry reflects credit on yourself but gives a very good idea of what people are thinking. It is that Waterperry is doing a really worthwhile job, but what happens if or when Miss Havergal ceases to be its directing spirit? With your own reputation so completely established and unchallengeable, would it help to wave the flag as it were, about the qualities, qualifications and experience of some of the senior members of your staff? Could they be brought or driven into the limelight?'

The Principals toyed with the idea of turning Waterperry into a charitable Trust but caution, and extremely good advice from the President of the RHS in his capacity as a friend, fortunately prevented this. Charitable Trust status might have induced support from Authorities who disliked all totally independent schools and colleges but could have looked more favourably on an institution managed by a board of governors with accounts available for inspection. But once a Trust was formed it belonged to its trustees, could not have been used as a financial asset for the Principals in later years and, far worse, they would have no control. In this context Miss H. wrote to the President, 'I would far rather sell Waterperry outright for some other cause than see it go downhill or fail in its objective.'

Even as the memorandum as to Waterperry's future was being considered another similar establishment, Studley Horticultural College for Women, was being closed. A friendly rivalry had existed over the years, and Miss H. would have remembered Lily Hughes Jones's exultant letter following the examination results in 1920, 'We have beaten Studley.' Now Studley was swept away, victim of the same economic and political forces that threatened Waterperry, and the estate bought by British Leyland Ltd. for a sum in excess of £200,000. These assets, since Studley had been registered with the Department of Education and Science as an educational charity, were to go into a Trust, to be used for any form of education in agriculture, horticulture, or similar subjects. Miss H., while genuinely dismayed at the closure, lost no time in writing to the Governors stressing Waterperry's financial needs. She received a sympathetic answer but no promise of assistance.

While these efforts were being made the partners themselves were losing ground. Miss S. wanted to retire, and she must have longed for a few years free of a mansion full of young women, their vagaries and, above all, their meals. In November 1969 she was suffering from high blood pressure and was away until the following January. For a time she rallied but was again admitted to hospital in Oxford, and on 20th August, 1970, this courageous, loyal and self-effacing woman died in her sleep at the age of seventy-five. The bell of Waterperry Church was tolled for her by Joan Stokes who felt that she could think about Miss S. as she rang the traditional sequence, six for a woman and seventy-five for the years of her life. She was buried in the churchyard on the north side beside Stephen Collingwood-Selby, Miss H.'s nephew, while Miss H. herself bore up heroically, shaking hands with every person who attended the funeral. A housekeeper had been installed during Miss S.'s illness, a small group of students was entered for September and the work went on.

Miss H., surrounded though she was by a devoted and capable staff and supported by her brother and sister, would nevertheless have been extremely lonely if she had not found one particular person to whom she could turn. Her cousin, Cynthia Havergal, a retired Headmistress living in Dorset, came over to Waterperry out of sheer goodness of heart to comfort her. Contact between the cousins formerly had been tenuous, and the only correspondence of any length was as far back as 1955 when Cynthia had sought help in the replanning of the school garden at St Audries in West Quantoxhead, and had been the recipient of much good advice and a price list of herbaceous plants, costing approximately one shilling and sixpence each. Now fifteen years later she was to become her cousin's sheet-anchor, the one person to whom she turned in the last troubled years of her life, and who had seemingly inexhaustible reserves of patience, compassion and understanding.

The early months of 1971 were marked by last-ditch efforts to find a solution to Waterperry's problems. For the first time for years Miss H. had to refuse a stand at Chelsea, and she had a consoling letter from the President, Lord Aberconway. 'The Show will not be the same without you, and certainly not so good . . . but it is wise to yield to the inevitable, sad though it is.' A Steering Committee was formed under the chairmanship of Sir Paul Sinker, a former Director-General of the British Council and another of Miss H.'s cousins, but no solution was forthcoming. The unfortunate first year students were told that they would not be able to complete their Waterperry training, and the whole estate was for sale on the open market.

Possible buyers came and went, and rumours of course abounded, the favourite being that Waterperry was to become a country club, and the gardens converted into a golf-course. The Institute of Flower Arrangers was certainly interested, and the British Leyland Motor Corporation, having already swallowed Studley, seemed quite keen to devour its sister. Eventually the real contenders were whittled down to two rather similar associations, both concerned with educational and philosophical movements with roots in Eastern thought, and both obviously attracted by the Waterperry ethos of dedication and hard work. The Subud movement, considering Waterperry as its future National Centre, showed a rather touching humility towards its possible inheritance. The definite offer for the estate was conditional, according to the *Subud News*, on that 'we would be competent to carry on the Waterperry tradition for excellence in the horticultural world.' The writer continued, 'This is the crux of the Waterperry concept. As one enters the gate one knows that here is an enterprise which has been the long preoccupation of the past forty years of a group of devoted people. Every plant in the ground and in the greenhouses proclaims this loving care, this spiritual link with the soil. If we buy Waterperry this preoccupation and this link will be our heritage. Waterperry is a place to love — it needs love and it gives it back.' The task for Subud would have been lightened by the fact that Miss H.'s staff would stay on, at any rate for a time. Certainly the Subuds would have loved Waterperry; it seems less likely that they could have coped with the harsh realities. The other contenders were the School of Economic Science from London, an educational charity with members world-wide, and attracting students from all walks of life, trades and professions. They needed Waterperry as replacement for a large house leased in Surrey and used extensively for residential courses. One personal factor was certainly in their favour, namely that one of Miss H.'s nephews was a member at that time and very keen for the deal to go through. This apart, the School of Economic Science had the resources in manpower that would be needed to put the place to rights. In August, 1971, this school became the new owner of Waterperry and the Horticultural School ceased to exist.

The price paid for the house and entire estate seems ludicrous compared with the inflated property values of today; at the time of writing it would not be sufficient to buy old Clifford's cottage at the end of the drive. However, although the grounds were in splendid order the house was in very poor shape and, in places, almost dangerous; over the years the few profits had been ploughed back, quite literally, into the land. The settlement also allowed Miss H. the use of one of the Mount

Spinney cottages, rent free, for as long as she should need it, a generous gesture and one that was readily accepted. Clearly Miss H. could not live alone, and Joan Stokes shelved her own plans to return to her native Shropshire and, with the dog Laddie, joined her in the cottage. The last Christmas cards to be sent to former students from the house, involving the usual seasonal marathon for staff of ensuring that Miss H. got down to the task in time, contained the words of a favourite hymn, 'Forth in Thy Name, O Lord, I go', and by Christmas Day the School of Economic Science had taken possession.

It seems fair to say that both parties must have been disappointed with some results of the transaction. The school — or SES as it is usually called — undoubtedly expected Miss H. to be able and willing to advise them over improvements and alterations, as some 'quid pro quo' for the cottage. In May she wrote excitedly to Cynthia that she had been round the gardens with Mr Maclaren, son of the founder and present head of the school, and that he had indicated that the school wished to use ideas she had had in the past. 'We could see the pattern of the large rock and water garden we had planned beyond the bridge and they want to carry my plan out with my help. It is so wonderful to think that one's early dreams of the place "made beautiful" may come true. The tutors are all so charming.' That particular part of the dream is still unfulfilled, and the SES probably failed at the outset to realize that Miss H. was fast losing the ability to concentrate, and would play no further part in the development of Waterperry. On the other hand Miss H. was grieved to find that the newcomers' way of life was somewhat alien to the quiet atmosphere of the last forty years. On a January Sunday in 1973 she wrote, again to Cynthia, 'It was a nice service but so few families and no one from the SES. I wish they didn't work on Sundays. It seems to be their principal day, and car after car comes past the cottage.'

The school certainly had their work cut out with repairs to the house, let alone the buildings. One of their first tasks, perhaps symbolic of a new regime, was to remove the all-enveloping creeper that had been so much a feature, and which had crept inside the window frames and wrapped itself lovingly round the balustraded parapet on the roof. Pessimists who swore that the entire building might collapse without its leafy corset were, fortunately, proved wrong, but much of the stone balustrading and the whole front facing had to be replaced. Sir John Curson would have been delighted with the result, the house emerging to show the original clean lines, though many former inhabitants mourned the passing of the familiar creeper.

Meanwhile the garden staff waited somewhat apprehensively to see what the future held. With the exception of the Collingwood-Selbys who retired to Cornwall and so made room for Miss H. to have the cottage, every member of staff was retained and the shop in the Oxford market continued as usual. Jean Manger was appointed Manager with Mary Spiller as her Deputy, and they had the difficult task of reconciling two very different outlooks. The gardeners, used to working steadily for long periods under a single command, and trained to consider thrift a virtue and the tools of their trade to be beyond price, found themselves sharing with strangers, members of a complicated hierarchy — certainly as many chiefs as indians — well-meaning but impulsive workers who, because of the short periods of time at their disposal, seemed to abandon many half-completed projects and who, through ignorance, used precious tools for purposes for which they were never intended. Worst of all, they were extravagant. It could have been a recipe for disaster. Fortunately both 'sides' had exactly the same objective, to give Waterperry a future while losing as little as possible of the best aspects of the past.

Whether it was wise for Miss H. to remain 'on the place' is a purely academic question. She had really little option seeing that she had a home for life, and she was treated with the utmost courtesy and respect by members of the school. But, sadly, with so much round her that could have brightened her last years, the enthusiasm and the physical well-being were missing. She could seldom be persuaded to walk round the gardens, though on her rare expeditions she was invariably delighted that standards were being maintained, and she never really lost interest. Occasionally she expresses her feelings in letters to Cynthia. 'Jean Manger was teaching a small group during the week how to prune apple trees. I walked into the lab with her this morning and saw some lovely branches of apple, all from one year up to six and eight years old, perfect examples of the natural development of an apple branch. One look at them gave me such a great desire to give them a talk on the building of an apple tree. Jean is obviously loving being able to do the demonstrating and lecturing. What a blessing for her that she always prepared for my talks by collecting the branches according to my lists. She didn't offer the job to me. I wish I could be a fly on the wall listening to her lecture . . . she can do beautiful work and is a real craftsman.' In the same year, 1973, *The Grower*, the RHS magazine, celebrating its Golden Jubilee published twelve photographs of 'Architects of Modern Horticulture' comprised of eleven men and Beatrix Havergal. Delighted, she wrote to Cynthia, 'I feel I still belong to horticulture. Eventually even attendance at church seemed to defeat her, although she clung tenaciously to the office of churchwarden. The Hammond organ presented in memory of Avice Sanders, a marvellous replacement for the old harmonium, should have given her hours of enjoyment, but sadly she never played it.

There were happy days of course; Cynthia Havergal — Havergal Two as she was affectionately called by the staff — saw to that. In the year following the sale the two cousins had a holiday in Tangiers, Miss H. rather anxiously having to acquire a different wardrobe. In 1973 they spent a delightful fortnight with Annalise Burchhardt-Reinhart in Winterthur, and exchanged memories of the never-to-be-forgotten Pusey days. She also stayed with the Collingwood-Selbys in Cornwall, and found that her rich contralto had not lost its power as far as the seals were concerned. 'They were lying tummies up on distant rocks, but when I started on hymn singing they all dived in and came over — seven delightful faces out of the water,' she wrote to Cynthia. She spent several weeks each year with her brother and his wife near Newbury, and Joan Stokes was her faithful companion at home. Former students who called in received a loving welcome, and she could always recall details of the past with the old enthusiasm and pleasure.

Beatrix Havergal died during the night of 7th April, 1980 at the age of seventy-nine, while visiting her brother. She was brought back to her beloved Waterperry on 14th April, her garden staff waiting at the drive entrance to pay a final tribute and following the coffin as it was driven slowly up to the church. She rests in the quiet churchyard with Avice Sanders, her friend and helpmeet for so many years.

Many tributes were paid to her, and the affectionate Obituary notice in *The Times*, written by Sir David Scott, deserves quotation in full.

> From *The Times*, 12th April, 1980.
> MISS BEATRIX HAVERGAL.
> A friend writes:
>
> There must be countless garden owners in this country who have reason to be grateful to Miss Beatrix Havergal, who died on April 8th. In 1931 she founded the Waterperry Horticultural School and, until it changed hands in 1971, turned out a steady stream of women gardeners, highly skilled in all branches of practical horticulture and imbued with habits of hard work.
>
> As a trainer in field work and as a lecturer she was unsurpassed, and a prominent head of department at Kew used to say that he would accept without question any applicant for employment who

had been at Waterperry.

Kindly and benevolent, Miss Havergal was yet a redoubtable figure who dominated her surroundings and would have stood out in any company, dressed as she invariably was in a green linen smock surmounted by a dark green blazer, with green breeches and green wool stockings, a white shirt and brown tie, and a dark brown hat.

By example and sheer personality she inspired her staff and students to accept without question a spartan regime, with work starting at 7 a.m., winter and summer, no tea breaks, and no question of payment for overtime. The spirit of the whole place indeed was such that it never occurred to anybody employed there that this was not a perfectly normal way of working.

Her great day came every May at the Chelsea Flower Show when she presided, a majestic figure, over the stand of the famous Waterperry strain of Royal Sovereign strawberries, every berry of which, whatever the weather had been, was invariably in perfect condition. It was the custom for the stand to be visited by the royal party in their perambulation round the show, and for a consignment of the fruit to be sent to Buckingham Palace.

Her later years were clouded by illness, but she will be remembered by all horticulturists as one of the leading figures of her time in the widely-spread world of gardening. For her work in the field of horticultural education she was appointed an MBE, and the Royal Horticultural Society granted her their highest award, the Victoria Medal of Honour, a very rare distinction for a woman.

Chapter Sixteen

When Beatrix Havergal left Waterperry House just before Christmas in 1971 Waterperry Horticultural School ceased to exist. Many mourned its passing, both those who had been closely associated and those who appreciated the high standards it had engendered. As a training centre it was unique, and is likely to remain so. But there was every hope that Waterperry itself, under its new owners but with Miss H.'s devoted staff, could continue in some form. It had two considerable assets, a name for excellent produce and the beautiful surroundings capable of providing that produce. Formerly it was only a name to many, either a cloistered community that could be entered rarely, and then only by invitation or a pleasant and helpful Market Shop. This had to change, but the School of Economic Science were prepared to give the gardeners time and a reasonably free hand to find a solution; Miss H.'s staff had the continuation of their jobs as incentive, if indeed any incentive was needed, to make things work.

To everyone's pleasure the *raison d'être* of Waterperry, its teaching aspect, was encouraged and continued. The contract of sale stipulated that the amateur classes should continue for at least another five years after the closure with Mary Spiller as lecturer. About twenty years on, the enthusiasm for horticultural instruction shows no sign of abating, and Mary, with the co-operation of Tom Farrer, the County Adviser, runs regular courses with exciting titles such as 'Enjoy your Garden' 'The Connoisseurs' Garden', or reassuringly 'Down to Earth'. Class members come in all shapes and sizes as before, very much as the Guinea Pigs with their stout hearts and strong boots. Twice a week Tom Farrer and an assistant instruct Day Release Students, complementing the knowledge these young men and women are already gaining in their jobs and preparing them for City and Guild examinations. In these days of redundancy older people often join them with the intention of launching out into a new career. A line of measured plots running across near the great sycamore tree are constantly being dug, prepared, planted or sown in attempts to gain the necessary skills, and the long polythene tunnel provides covered conditions in bad weather.

But these students, while preserving valuable continuity with the past, could not replace the young women who both studied their subject and provided the labour while paying for the privilege. Changes had to be made if the new venture was to succeed, and these had to take into account economic factors, changes in fashion, and social patterns. The most radical of these changes affected the walled garden and its intensive vegetable crops grown under cloches, so orderly and attractive, and so costly to maintain. It was eventually transformed in one day by a tractor and earth-moving machinery, and the superb soil, hand-worked, cosseted and enriched over the years, disappeared for ever under sheets of plastic and gravel paths. Viewers of an excellent BBC production of The Victorian Kitchen Garden will have some inkling of the growing skills, the ingenuity and the enthusiasms that have disappeared with the soil. The Waterperry walled garden is, at present, a standing-out area for container-grown shrubs in different stages of their development, displaying attractive variations of colour, shape and texture. Trained fruit on the warm brick walls, and herb beds, still keep faith with tradition.

Another department to have felt the wind of change is the Glass, partly through the ever rising cost of heating old houses and partly because of changing fashion and tastes. The green plant revolution, so well summed up by Flanders and Swann in their song 'A Design for Living' — 'the garden's full of furniture and the house is full of plants' seems to have come to stay and customers are no longer content with the simple and colourful cineraria or primula. It may be that stark contemporary architecture has contributed to the popularity of the ubiquitous rubber plant or the 'mother-in-law's tongue'. The handsome new Sales House therefore has to include more than a little 'bought-in' material and exotics, while the older houses have the air of shabby but aristocratic types faced by a somewhat *nouveau riche* colleague. But the orange tree, one of the First Causes, remains to fascinate present visitors, and is acquiring much the same status as that attributed to the apes of Gibraltar, symbols of continuity.

Beyond the walled garden the ornamental and utilitarian live happily together. However gardens seldom stand still, and many species have only a limited life-span. For example, Miss H.'s treasured rose-border, planted with such delight in 1968 had, for years, delighted the senses when in bloom, and had often provided class material on which amateurs could practise their pruning techniques. Refurbishment and realignment of the sheltering hedge after Miss H.'s death improved the design but could not halt the ageing process. All bushes and the aromatic border of lavender were eventually taken out, and the area is presently grassed down for a period to allow the soil to recover before replanting with roses.

Alan Bloom's island beds, by contrast, only require occasional refurbishment, and the herbaceous nursery beside them still remains the most orderly part of the South Field, thanks to the tireless hoeing of Helen Williams, the doyen of the female staff. The longest serving member of the staff as a whole is Stefan Lanczak who, having taken refuge in this country from Poland, joined the West Field team in 1955 and married Josie Munday, the daughter of Mrs O'Connor's chauffeur. He is now a British subject and works in the Fruit Department with son Christopher, the present Head of the Department. Much of the fruit is to be found in the West Field but the cordons once measured out by moonlight still stride down the South Field and are constantly being replanted. The long stretch of grass running down from the dining room windows has been improved considerably with the planting of a long shrub border beside the drive down towards Waterstock and with the imaginative creation of a curved bed of dwarf and prostrate conifers.

The latest project is still in its infancy but promises to be full of interest. An enclosed garden has been designed in the lower part of the Herbaceous nursery, its surrounding hedge of yew already about three feet high and growing well. Features so far include a climber covered pergola, Elizabethan knot, 'chronological' beds displaying plants discovered or developed in successive centuries, and a large herb bed.

The house remains somewhat aloof now that no eager workers go out and in daily for meals and study, though it is frequently bursting at the seams at weekends. The last horticultural foothold was lost when the old safe, proof against mice and damp and so ideal for seed storage, was swept away in the building of a new staircase, new but actually a replacement for one in Curson days. The narrow wooden stairs, down which bleary-eyed students stumbled in their quest for the morning thermoses, are now things of the past. For a time the Garden Office remained in the house; now it is to be found in the end of Miss Kitson's teaching block, a far more accessible position. Another rather strange little building near it, known as 'The Ark' acts as an office for the Garden Manager and the Deputy; it provides a splendid vantage point to watch over comings and goings, but is not infrequently mistaken for an ice-cream kiosk. Comings and goings there are in plenty as visitors come to the Garden Shop and Sales Area. The shop, from its modest beginnings, has grown out of all recognition and threatens to absorb the marketing shed where students once sang as they sorted strawberry plants in their thousands. Shrubs and fruit trees, with tables for Alpine plants and herbs stand where once bullocks were fattened and where manure heaps were turned for the hot beds.

Once a year the house and gardens together are caught up in a totally different whirl of activity when the SES stages its Art in Action Festival. Marquees mushroom overnight in the Warren and on the lawns, and Waterperry is invaded by artists and craftsmen whose skills range from calligraphy to carpet-weaving, from glass-blowing to sculpture. For four days they demonstrate these skills to a fascinated public, prepared to answer any questions about their methods while they work, and the programme includes the performing arts such as theatre and music. The whole event is superbly organized by the SES though they have not yet succeeded in controlling the weather. The Festival was originally held in May until one memorable year when rain fell incessantly, turning the ground between the marquees into quagmire despite the ten tons of straw spread about by the garden staff. The grass did not recover until the late autumn. Art in Action has now moved to July and has flourished, despite one year when it was unbelievably too hot for good attendance, and there was another dramatic opening coinciding exactly with a mighty clap of thunder and a cloudburst. Both garden staff and villagers brace themselves for this annual 'happening' endure or enjoy it according to temperament and outlook, and sink back, aesthetically enriched but with some relief, when it is over. The gardens, quite rightly, play second fiddle to the exhibitions on this occasion, but exhausted visitors take refuge there for a few moments before plunging back into the throng; many of these return on quieter days to enjoy them to the full.

On 16th June, 1985, a very different gathering took place at Waterperry when a Horticultural School Reunion was held with the generous encouragement of the SES. The event was the end result of considerable industry shown by Jenny Woods in Edinburgh, who set out to discover what had been happening to her contemporaries in training from 1953 to 1956. She intended to confine herself to those three years but the operation snowballed until she had produced a comprehensive booklet containing the names and, hopefully, the addresses of nearly all the former staff and students with potted biographies supplied by many of the subjects. This was a real labour of love since the only source of information, Miss H.'s old address book, was woefully out of date, and it gave real impetus to the idea of a reunion. The response to an invitation was excellent and many former students, together with husbands and children, gathered on the lawn, were labelled to make recognition easier after the passage of time and set free to renew old friendships, fill in the gaps, and find out exactly what had happened to Waterperry. It was a very nostalgic occasion. In the centre of the marquee stood the Hardaker portrait of Miss H., loaned by Commander Havergal and making a remarkable impact on all who had known the original so well. The Commander, so like his sister in appearance and manner, was there with his wife, together with Cynthia, 'Havergal Two'. It had been hoped that Miss S.'s surviving sister, Joan Sanders, would be present, but she was not well enough to come. But Miss Kitson who had been influenced by a robin was there, voluntarily released from anonymity, and so was the Downe House friend who had made the purchase possible. Over tea Jean Manger and Mary Spiller welcomed everyone, introduced the guests of honour, and paid tribute to the SES for their patience and help in steering Waterperry into new channels.

Several of the early 'stalwarts' were at the Reunion and, of these, Joan Stokes seemed her inimitable self, delighted to be back in such familiar surroundings. Those close to her knew that she had heart trouble but no one was prepared for the news, only a fortnight later, that she had died suddenly early one morning in her precious new garden. In retrospect the Reunion was a fitting occasion for her farewell to Waterperry, surrounded by so many friends. Several of the Waterperry staff attended her funeral in the little church at Trefonen, near Oswestry and she lies in a quiet green churchyard close to her home. Afterwards they were privileged to visit the garden she had made high on a Shropshire hillside and found, as expected, everything in perfect order. Other 'stalwarts' at the Reunion included a rather more matronly 'Dobber' Rosemary Meredith, and Valerie Finnis, (Lady Scott), sporting the Alpine style hat with upturned brim that was her trademark when working in the nursery. The day was indeed a time for excited recognitions, revisiting every part of the gardens and buildings, and being reassured that Waterperry was still in capable hands and was in good heart.

The place has seen many changes over this century and no doubt will continue to evolve, bracing itself to meet pressures from within and without. No one can predict what the effect will be now that the long threatened motorway, the M40, is being built. This is destroying the hitherto unspoilt countryside around, and cuts across the road from Wheatley to Waterperry, the Centre's main artery, with all the noise and pollution motorways invariably bring. So far Waterperry has weathered the change from Horticultural School to Horticultural Centre reasonably well. In the spring of '89 tradition was broken with the appointment of Jonathan Cooke as Manager, the first man to take command of Waterperry. Mary Spiller continues to watch over the Flower Garden and teach the amateur classes. The managership is not an easy assignment, caught between the high standards of the past and the present pressures of commercialization, while the School of Economic Science, for all its good intentions, remains alien in some respects. Regrettably, but inevitably, there has been loss of variety of activity and of produce, together with precious and now almost forgotten skills. Rare too is the comprehensive knowledge inherent in the Waterperry training and which few of the present staff can claim to possess. On the credit side many families can now enjoy the grounds, relax over a cup of tea or a simple meal while the children play on the grass and, hopefully, return home refreshed with a Waterperry plant or two to enrich their own gardens.

The unique atmosphere in the gardens themselves has not altered and is remarked on by many on their first visit and who have no knowledge of the enterprise from its beginnings. The writer has talked with many people in the preparation of this history, and she asked one former student how she would explain why Waterperry has this very special 'feel'. "Because it was created with so much love," was the reply, and surely that is the explanation. At the centre of it all is the church of St Mary the Virgin, witness to a changeless and greater Love, and from which both Beatrix Havergal and Avice Sanders derived strength. In 1988, following the statutory interval after Beatrix Havergal's death a plaque to her memory was placed on the north wall near her organ, and facing the memorial to her friend. It reads:

> In loving memory of Beatrix Havergal, M.B.E., V.M.H. who lived at Waterperry House from 1932 to 1972, and with her partner, Avice Sanders, founded the School of Horticulture. She dedicated her life to imparting to others her great faith, her joy, and her unique skills.

Appendix (i)

Waterperry Horticultural School: 1937 Prospectus

Aims of the School

It is the object of the School to provide the theoretical foundation, the practical knowledge of Horticulture and the specialized skill required to make a first-class gardener, and in addition to this, the development of the qualities of organization necessary for the management of a small or large staff of under-gardeners.

It is important to realize that in the construction and management of a small garden as much skill and knowledge is required as in the management of a large garden which may have been laid out and prepared generations ago.

There is, in these days, scope for the Jobbing gardener, the Market gardener, and for the highly qualified Landscape gardener, and the training at Waterperry includes all that is necessary to enable a girl to take up any of these careers, or any other specific branch of horticultural work. Great stress is laid on individual work, and at the same time care is taken that the strength of any student should not at any time be overtaxed.

It is sometimes forgotten that an educated girl cannot be only a gardener, and the proximity of Oxford affords an opportunity to the students to develop their intellectual and artistic interests, a point which is often ignored when Horticultural training is considered. There are choirs, orchestras, lectures and libraries, and an intellectual society of which students are encouraged to avail themselves.

Course of Study

This extends over a period of three years, but the lectures are so arranged as to enable a student, if not wishing to be a professional, to take one or two years only. Short courses can be arranged in any special subject if desired.

FIRST YEAR

The general principles of all subjects which will provide a real foundation for further study:

Propagation. Seed and vegetative in all forms, plant raising, watering, etc.

Management of glasshouses and frames, including ventilation, stoking, etc.

Management and manipulation of all tools.

Soils, origin, composition, and characteristics.

Manures, organic and inorganic.

Botany. The elements of morphology — structure of cells, anatomy of roof, leaf, and stem; structure and function of various tissues;

Elements of physiology, composition of the plant; absorption of water, ascent of sap; transpiration; manufacture of foods; storage; respiration; fermentation; work of bacteria in relation to plant nutrition, conditions affecting germination and growth of seeds.

Pruning — all kinds of growth, including shrubs; the training of fruit trees from propagation to the mature tree.

Fruit. Hardy and under glass. Soft fruit, bush and tree fruits, and general management.

Flowers. Construction of herbaceous and shrub borders including lawns, care of rose, iris, rock, wild and water gardens. The propagation and general treatment of annuals, biennials and perennials.

Vegetables. General management and cropping of Kitchen Garden on market and private lines. Cultural details of the principal groups of vegetables, e.g. salad, root, and legume crops, and the forcing of vegetables out of season.

Pests and Diseases — general principles of control.

SECOND YEAR

The student will go into each of the above subjects more fully and lectures are given on the individual fruits, flowers and vegetables under glass and in the open. Botany is continued throughout the course. Students will be prepared for the Royal Horticultural Society's General Examination, taken at the end of the Second Year.

THIRD YEAR

Students are advised to concentrate on the general management of a garden, and to make a special study of fruit and vegetables, and to specialize in any branch of the work in which she is particularly interested.

MARKETING SECTION

As the gardens supply fruit and vegetables to many customers in Oxford, including Colleges, Students have excellent opportunities of learning first-class market gardening. All kinds of cut flowers and plants have to be grown during the year to meet increasing demands of the stall in Swindon Market. Students play an important part in this work and, in their second and third years, take responsibility and manage, with expert guidance, the routine work of the gardens. The instruction is supplemented by visits to the Royal Horticultural Society's gardens at Wisley, Research stations, and principal Horticultural Shows.

RECREATIONS

Tennis, badminton, boating, golf, etc.

FEES: Inclusive, board and tuition.

Study bedroom.	£120 per annum.
Ordinary bedroom.	£100-£110 p.a.
Double room.	£95-£100
Tuition only.	£14 per term.

SESSIONS: Three terms of approximately 13 weeks each.

Appendix (ii)

OUR APPLE EXHIBIT — RHS AUTUMN FRUIT SHOW, 7th OCTOBER 1952

Written by Beatrix Havergal for the RHS Fruit Year Book in April, 1953.

It is one of the most exciting things to pick the first really good crop of apples on young trees that one has planted and tended from earliest infancy. We had this excitement in September 1952, when three acres of young bushes, planted in 1946, came into real bearing for the first time. This meant that quite a number of varieties, both culinary and dessert, would be available to add to our collection. The avenue of cordon trees and some older bushes, also, were bearing well, and two long rows of young pyramid trees had a wonderful crop for the first time.

When the fruit began to colour I began to take it seriously and saw visions of an exhibit at the Autumn Fruit Show, but I was afraid the colour would not be good enough. Fortunately during the month there was quite a lot of sunshine and we escaped the high winds which so often bruise and mark the fruit, and by the end of September we had picked some wonderfully nice apples. In order to get the highest colour, each variety was left until the fruit literally dropped into the hand, and only the best apples were graded into trays — in single rows, making two grades, large and medium of each variety. The trays were stacked in the fruit-room in readiness for the final sorting, and coloured chalk lettering on the end of each tray indicated the variety and grade. During the week before the Show it was necessary to pick over the later varieties, and, when finished, there were 33 varieties of dessert and 16 of culinary apples, and 3 varieties of pears, with anything from two to fifteen trays of each variety.

We applied for, and were granted, a table space of 24 feet by 6 feet, with a background, and hastily began to plan the exhibit. Its main purpose was not only to display the collection of varieties to the best possible advantage and to make an attractive picture, but also to accentuate the characteristic points of difference — such as size, shape and colour — between each variety, points which are both interesting and important. One is always rather proud of the large culinary apples, and bold groups of well-chosen Bramleys, Warner's King, Newton Wonder, and many others make a splendid contrast amongst the ideal medium-sized dessert apples. Some are round and 'bulgy', others are beautifully conical in shape, and the colours are wonderfully varied. By careful arrangement these differences can be accentuated and appreciated.

Then came the question of a good background. There can be little doubt that black velvet behind the fruit not only shows up the colour admirably but provides a dignity which is a point worth considering when putting up an exhibit. So often black cotton material is used, which has gone rather grey with constant use, and one has only to put a few rich green or red apples on a piece of black velvet to realize its enormous value. Unfortunately it is expensive but once purchased it should last for years.

The next point to consider was the actual arrangement of the apples, whether to use the orthodox baskets or to build directly on to the velvet. I have never liked baskets but really enjoy the pyramid-shaped groups. These are difficult to build unless the apples are carefully graded to one size, and in this respect I suffered considerable anxiety. The students had done so much of the grading, and it was difficult for them, without previous experience, to realize the importance of such careful selection; one or two misshapen fruit will throw out the symmetry of the pyramid, but with a little practice and provided the apples are packed closely together, each layer rests comfortably, ending with one apple on top. The effect of a well built pyramid is rather striking. In order to make an attractive colour scheme, a list was made of the varieties available, grouping the culinary and dessert separately under their respective colours, and from these lists it was easy to see how many of each colour were available.

A few nights before the Show, when playing with a pencil and a scale plan, I decided to divide the 24 foot length of the exhibit into three sections, each 8 foot long, and to fill the middle section with the most popular and highly-coloured dessert varieties, hoping to make an attractive centre-piece. Looking lengthways, there were to be four lines of pyramids, each tier to be 18 inches wide and the back tier to be 3 feet 6 inches above the table.

Then came the packing. Each apple was carefully wrapped in tissue paper and held firm in the tray with wood-wool to prevent bruising, the end of each tray being clearly marked with name and grade. On the

Sunday morning before the Show, I spent a very pleasant time cutting bold sprays of Cotoneaster salicifolia, rich in small scarlet berries, to furnish either side of the exhibit, and shorter sprays of the most attractive pale green-leaved Berberis pruinosa, with its small silvery-blue berries, for a vase in the centre. We set off to London on the Sunday evening, with the lorry well and truly loaded with the trays and background material and on arrival at the Hall we unloaded, stacking the trays in neat piles in readiness for the morning. We began work at 8.30 on Monday morning, full of excitement but secretly alarmed at the conspicuous position of our table.

The three-tier staging required considerable levelling and adjustment, and to break the otherwise long and uneventful lines of the two back tiers we arranged a 6-inch drop in the centre of both, 4 foot wide for the back, to accommodate the vase of Berberis pruinosa, and five foot wide in the second line to make a rather special place for the bold group of Cox's Orange Pippins in the centre.

Once the 24 foot length of black velvet (purchased for the occasion) was pinned in position to make the background, and the back tier was covered with a narrow strip of velvet, the vase of Berberis was arranged and the building of the pyramids began. Using drawing pins as markers, we placed one vital pin to mark the centre of the exhibit, from which we worked on either side, putting a pin at every 3 foot to mark the centre of the tall pyramids. We then built the six tall pyramids of culinary apples, choosing Warner's King and Bramley Seedling on either side of the centre, and Lord Derby and Arthur Turner at either end to provide a green effect, and midway between them we had the scarlet-flushed Monarch and Gascoigne's Scarlet, which made an excellent contrast in colour. Between the large pyramids we built smaller pyramids of medium-sized apples. On either side of the Berberis pruinosa, in the 4 foot centre space, we built two small pyramids of the most highly coloured red dessert apples to make a good contrast to the green apples on either side, using American Mother and Laxton's Fortune.

We then prepared the second tier, measuring as before, but this time the tallest pyramids of large apples alternated with those at the back, so creating a balance. In the centre our largest Cox's Orange Pippins formed a bold oval-shaped group, with small groups of Russet apples on either side. We continued this scheme of alternating large and small groups, varying the colours and shapes of the apples, until we reached the front of the table and, here, smaller groups of dessert apples completed the picture. The tall branches of Cotoneaster furnished the sides of the exhibit, and to soften the otherwise hard effect scarlet and green Ampelopsis leaves protruded from the base of each pyramid. As further decoration, short well-berried sprigs of different kinds of Berberis were laid between the pyramids.

The plan worked out surprisingly well, and when looking at it from a distance, I was delighted to find that there was an attractive colour scheme, thrown up by the rich black background, that the apples looked clean and unmarked, and that by varying the sizes of the groups we had avoided monotony which so often occurs when baskets of the same size are used throughout. Also, by careful measurement and spacing the exhibit appeared uncrowded, and there was regularity and precision which lent a dignity to the whole picture.

The fun of doing it was indescribable, and I think the five second-year students who came up to assist me, together with four members of my staff, enjoyed every minute in spite of the long twelve-hour day we spent in the Hall. There is no doubt whatever that putting up an exhibit of apples is a great entertainment, and the award of the Silver Gilt Hogg Medal was extremely encouraging.

Appendix (iii)

April 1966. 1st year Examination in Horticultural Operation. 2 Hours.

Four questions only to be answered.

1. Describe the process of fertilization in a flower such as the butter-cup.

Explain how the ovule subsequently becomes a seed. Illustrate with well labelled diagrams.

2. What is meant by

   a) Perennation.

   b) Vegetative propagation.

Give two examples of each process, and explain why they are important horticulturally.

3. Describe one method of sub-irrigation for pot plants, and outline the principles involved in this system of watering.
4. Write notes on the following:
   a) emasculation of a flower.
   b) insect pollination.
   c) dormancy in seeds.
   d) the importance of water in seed germination.
   e) pore space in soil.
   f) the transpiration stream.

5. What do you understand by the term 'family' in flowering plants? Illustrate your answer by drawing the half-flower of a member of a family of your own choosing, and discuss any other characteristics of this family which are of botanical or horticultural importance.

6. Answer briefly 3 of the following:
   a) How would you find the pH value of soil?
   b) Describe the value of bacteria to the family Papilionaceae.
   c) What are the effects of mulching?
   d) What is mole drainage, and where would you use it?

7.Describe fully how four of the following pests survive through the winter and what methods of control you would use at this stage.

a) Winter Moths.
b) Fruit tree red spider mite.
c) Pear Midge.
d) Blackcurrant Gall Mite.
e) Chrysanthemum leaf miner.

8. How would you produce a supply of cabbages all the year round? Mention suitable varieties with the times for sowing and planting. Briefly describe preparation of the ground.

9. Choose either Potato Root Eelworm or Cabbage Root Fly. Describe the symptoms caused by an attack, the life cycle, and how you would control.

10. Describe the methods you would adopt to produce a good lawn on a well drained level site from a) seed and b) turf.

11. Describe with diagrams the vegetative propagation of strawberries. Explain the importance of an up-to-date method of plant production.

12. Write notes on three of the following:
a) Raised beds.
b) Choice of plants for a shady site.
c) Planning a heather garden.
d) Planting a garden pool.

July 1966. First Year Practical Examination. 9.30 — 1 p.m.

Potting Shed

1. Sow the two kinds of seeds provided in a suitable soil mixture.
a) in pots, leaving half uncovered.
b) in a box, leaving half uncovered.
Label with your Number, and, if possible, name the seeds.

2. Prick out One box of the seedlings provided. Label with your Number.

3. From the material provided, C, D, E and F select suitable material for propagation. Prepare three examples of C, D, and E. Prepare, insert and complete 1 pan of F, using suitable rooting medium. Label with your Number.

4. Pot into suitable size pots the plants provided. Give particulars of the soil mixtures used. Label.

On the Plots

5. Prepare a seed bed, mark out for two rows 10 foot long of each of the seed provided. Sow 1 row of each, indicating with a peg the correct spacing of the second row of each. Name seed and label, leaving half the row uncovered.
6. Plant one row of each of the plants provided, and indicate with a peg the position of second rows. Name the plants with the labels provided.
7. Plant, stake, and tie the plant provided.
8. From material provided labelled A and B, select suitable cuttings, make and insert six cuttings of each in two rows at suitable spacing.

2.15 p.m.— 5 p.m.

9. Give generic, specific, and variety names of twenty of the specimens labelled 1-25 in the Laboratory. English and common names may be given.
10. Identify causes of trouble in the specimens A-E in the middle room. Give one accepted method of control with the quantity of chemicals recommended.
11. Name the substances used in horticulture labelled F-J in the Demonstration Room. Comment briefly on their uses.
12. On the numbered plot place two rows of each of the following in a workable arrangement — two rows of Raspberries, two Blackcurrant, two of Gooseberries, one row of Loganberries, one Cordon apples. Indicate in one row of each the spacing required. Label each fruit, suggesting the variety you would recommend.
13. Separate the mixture of seeds laid out. Name them and suggest one good variety and the season for use for each.
14. The plants in your plot are to be increased. Carry out an accepted method of propagation and plant as for one group in the Flower Garden.
15. On the seed sowing end of the plot mark out a rectangular border 6 foot by 10 foot. Prepare it for seed sowing and sketch a simple plan of an arrangement for 12 hardy annual flowers. Label the groups.

Examination for Waterperry Diploma. April 1967

Part One: answer 6 questions, one from each section

A. *Vegetables.*

1. Outline the cultivation of either a) Runner Beans or b) Cabbage as a market garden crop, under the headings: Propagation, Soil, site, and details of previous croppings, Fertilizer &/or manure, Planting out, with details of cultivation up to picking time, Varieties.
2. Much research and experimental work has recently gone into the improvement of vegetables. Using two specific crops of your own choice give an account of this and name some new varieties.

B. *Tree Fruit.*

1. Explain, with diagrams, four of the following: a) Double working, b) Renewal pruning, c) Pillar apple trees, d) Bark ringing, e) Summer pruning, f) Controlled atmosphere storage.
2. Write an essay on 'Spring pests in fruit growing' under the following headings: a) Behaviour of spring pests, b) Nature of damage, c) Importance of orchard site selection, d) prevention or reduction of damage.

C. *Flowers.*

1. Describe the construction of a rock garden, suitable for a small country garden. Name and briefly describe twelve plants that would be suitable.
2. Describe ornamental tree and shrub pruning under the headings Why — When — and How. Illustrate your answer with reference to named examples.

D. *Glass.*

1. What are the reasons for soil sterilization in glasshouses? Mention all the methods you know, and describe one in detail.
2. Write notes on a) all the year round Chrysanthemum b) Automatic watering c) Application of C02 to glasshouse crops d) Winter lettuce under glass.

E. *Pests.*

1. Describe the life history and damage caused by with control measures for 4 of the following a) Apple sawfly b) Narcissus fly c) Fruit tree red spider mite d) Black bean aphis e) Onion fly f) Chrysanthemum eelworm.
2. Describe, with examples, the main groups of chemicals used in horticulture for the control of insect pests. Discuss the advantages and disadvantages of the groups named.

F. *Soils.*

1. How would you create 'high fertility' in vegetable-growing soil? Discuss in the following aspects — Chemical, Physical, Biological and Cultural.
2. Discuss the use of irrigation in the growing of vegetables and mention any drawbacks. For two crops of your own choice state when, and how much water you would apply, and outline the method of application.

Part Two: Answer six questions, one from each section

G. *Diseases.*

1. Describe the visual symptoms by which you would recognize damage caused by the following: a) Fireblight b) Whiptail c) Silver leaf d) Cauliflower mosaic e) Verticillium wilt on tomatoes f) Honey fungus. Describe suitable control measures for 2 of these.
2. Excluding the use of chemicals, describe briefly various methods used in commercial horticulture for controlling plant diseases.

H. *Manures and Fertilizers.*

1. Give suitable fertilizer regimes, with reasons, for the following; Lawns — Spring and summer Cabbage — Strawberries — House Plants — Cold House tomatoes.
2. What is meant by the 'unit value' system of associated fertilizers, and of what practical use is it to a grower? Illustrate your answer by reference to at least two examples of compound fertilizers.

I. *Plant Physiology.*

1. Explain the importance of a) Light and b) Temperature to the various functions carried out by plants.
2. Distinguish between a) enzymes b) hormones. Explain the importance of both these types of substances to plants, and show how our knowledge of them can be applied in horticultural practice.

J. *Structural Botany.*

1. Describe the structure of the mature ovule in a flower at the time of fertilization. Assuming fertilization to be successful what changes will the ovule undergo. Illustrate with diagrams at all stages.
2. Give an account of the external features and internal tissue arrangement in a typical herbaceous stem as found in both Dicotyledons and Monocotyledons. What are the functions of the stem in herbaceous plants? Diagrams are essential.

K. *Soft Fruit.*

1. Outline in diary form a programme of work to be carried out during

the year on a fruiting plantation of either strawberries or raspberries. Pest and disease control should be included.

2. Commercial methods for soft fruit production have changed considerably during recent years. Describe various developments to support this statement.

L. *Weed control.*

1. Write short notes, with reference to weed killers, on the following terms a) Residual b) Contact c) Translocated d) Selective.

2. Give your recommendations — both cultural and chemical — for the preparation of a weed free seed bed.